Quilting never goes out of season. Enjoy!

Eleanor Burns

QUILTS
Through the Seasons

Eleanor Burns

For Esther, stylist from Benartex, Inc.

Thank you for bringing to life my beautiful fabric line, Through the Seasons. I can still hear you say in your charming New York accent, "Eleanor, your fabric is pret-ty and ladies like pret-ty!"

My Sincere Appreciation,

Eleanor Burns

I appreciate the dedication Esther and her associate, Jessica, gave to the beautiful *Through the Seasons* collection. I'm also grateful for the help Linda Parker and my sister, Patricia Knoechel, gave when I was unable to talk directly to the artists.

Most of the quilts featured are made using *Through the Seasons* fabrics. On the fabric selection pages, the numbers reference my line, so you too can find them easily in your local quilt shop. If you are unable to locate them, you may call Quilt in a Day.

Comments from Susan Neill, Marketing Director for Benartex, Inc.: "*Through the Seasons* contains all the elements for a beautiful quilt – lush oversized roses have a unique textured lace ground. They combine wonderfully with delicate rosebuds, mini checks and floral springs. The combination of scales and colors makes this group truly versatile, not only for quilting, but for home decorating as well. This is going to be a quilting classic!"

First Edition
April, 2006
Published by Quilt in a Day®, Inc.
1955 Diamond Street, San Marcos, CA 92078
©2006 by Eleanor A. Burns Family Trust

ISBN 1-891776-20-7

Art Director: Merritt Voigtlander
Production Artists: Marie Harper, Ann Huisman

Contents

Introduction

I love the seasons! As they change each year, the beds and walls in my Bear's Paw Ranch are stripped of familiar quilts and replaced with fresh, new ones. Dining table linens are traded for crisp new tablerunners. I bring the out-of-doors inside, decorating with the colors of the season in floral prints. I'm so fortunate to have my own fabric line, Through the Seasons, to decorate with… in four colorways no less!

In the spring, sunny yellow daffodils emerge under clear blue skies, and the meadows in Julian, California are covered with them. I head to the garden center, selecting deer and squirrel resistant plants. Soon, bluebell and butter yellow floral garlands grace my once bare windows. My home, decorated in soft spring colors speaks of renewal and refreshment!

During the summer the water temperature is perfect for snorkeling the sky blue Pacific Ocean, or for heading to Hawaii with my sons, Grant and Orion. At the "Ranch," huge American Beauty roses bloom in soft petal pinks. Willows grace my creek bed, with their slender, flexible branches. My wrap around porch becomes a haven for relaxation with a glass of pink lemonade. Inside the beds and walls glow with inviting Victorian cream and rose print quilts.

All too soon the breezes cool and the leaves begin to change color. In the fall, I love taking long walks down my country lane amidst falling leaves of liquid gold amber trees. Wild turkeys often accompany me. I wonder how an ol' turkey would look stuffed with apple and sage and gracing my harvest tablerunner. I'm the family cook for Thanksgiving, and I look forward to welcoming them into my home smoothed in colors of rich butternut, rust, and plum.

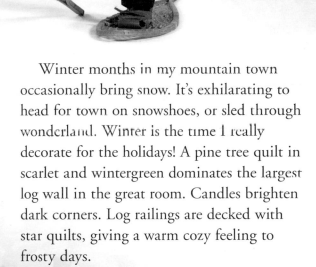

Winter months in my mountain town occasionally bring snow. It's exhilarating to head for town on snowshoes, or sled through wonderland. Winter is the time I really decorate for the holidays! A pine tree quilt in scarlet and wintergreen dominates the largest log wall in the great room. Candles brighten dark corners. Log railings are decked with star quilts, giving a warm cozy feeling to frosty days.

I do love decorating my home for the seasons and I believe changing the accents to celebrate each one will bring happiness to you, too. Won't you join me in this rewarding tradition?

Eleanor Burns

General Supplies

Using good tools will
increase your accuracy.

*Cut a piece of InvisiGRIP™ ½" smaller than ruler. Place on bottom
side of ruler. InvisiGRIP keeps the ruler from sliding when cutting.*

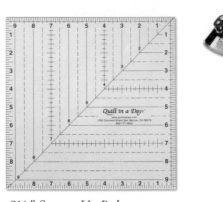

9½" Square Up Ruler

¼" Foot

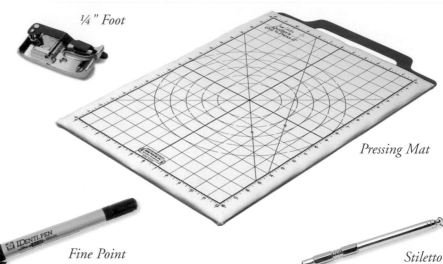

Pressing Mat

*Fine Point
Permanent
Marking Pen*

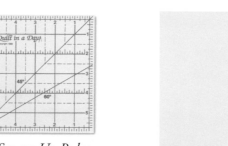

Stiletto

6" x 24" Ruler

*6½" Triangle
Square Up Ruler*

6" Square Up Ruler

Template Plastic

6" x 12" Ruler

4" x 14" Ruler

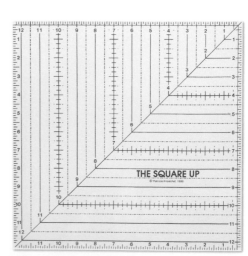

12½" Square Up Ruler

Applique Tools

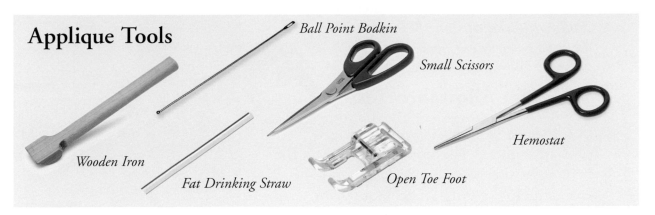

Ball Point Bodkin

Small Scissors

Hemostat

Wooden Iron

Fat Drinking Straw

Open Toe Foot

6" x 8" and 18" x 24" Cutting Mats
(not shown)

4" x 8" Large
Flying Geese Ruler

3" x 6" Small
Flying Geese Ruler

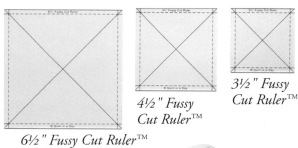

6½" Fussy Cut Ruler™

4½" Fussy
Cut Ruler™

3½" Fussy
Cut Ruler™

Rotary Cutter

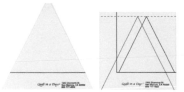

Triangle In a Square Rulers

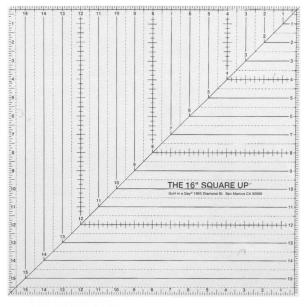

16" Square Up Ruler

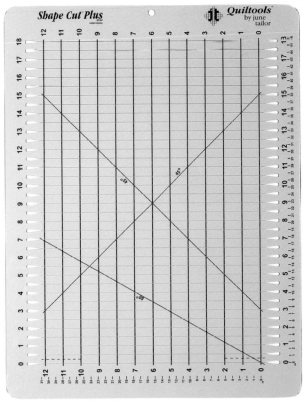

12" x 18" Shape Cut™ Plus

Following the tips on these pages will help you become a better quilter.

¼" Seam Allowance Test

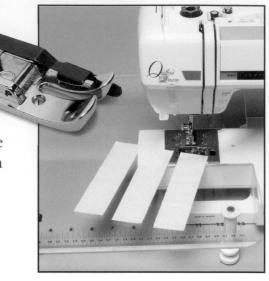

1. Place a ¼" foot on your sewing machine. A ¼" foot has a guide on the right side of it to help keep fabric from straying, giving an accurate seam. Patchwork is then consistent.

2. Cut three 1½" x 6" pieces.

3. Place a fine, sharp #70/10 needle on your machine. Set machine at 15 stitches per inch, or 2.0 on computerized machines.

4. Thread your machine with a good quality of neutral shade cotton or polyester spun thread.

5. Sew three strips together lengthwise with what you think is a ¼" seam.

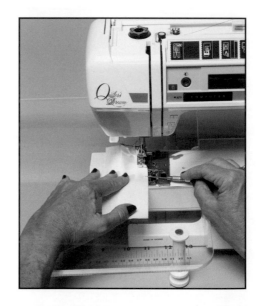

6. Press seams in one direction. Make sure no folds occur at seams.

7. Place sewn sample under a ruler and measure its width. It should measure exactly 3½". If sample measures smaller than 3½", seam is too wide. If sample measures larger than 3½", seam is too narrow. Adjust seam width by moving needle one or two threads to the left or right, and repeat if necessary.

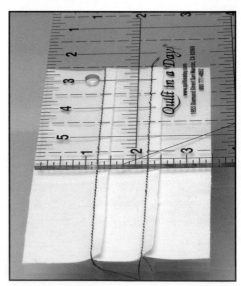

Pressing

1. Place fabric on pressing mat, with fabric on top that seam is to be pressed toward. Individual instructions say which way to press seams. Set seam by pressing stitches.

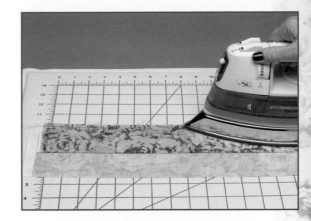

2. Open the fabric strips with your fingers, and press against seam with iron.

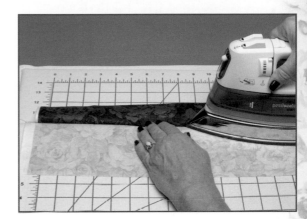

Measuring Your Bed

Decide if you want your quilt to cover just the sides of your top mattress or cover to the floor. Decide if you will tuck the pillows under the quilt or use pillow shams on top of the quilt. Measure the length and width of what you want covered on your bed.

Check the approximate finished sizes at the top of each yardage chart to find one that is closest to your desired size. You can design your own size by increasing or decreasing the number of blocks and the sizes and number of borders.

Measure to bottom edge of top mattress plus the drop to figure the size you desire.

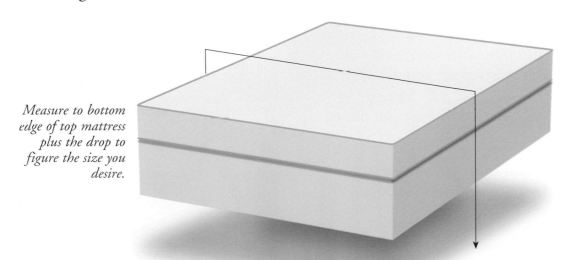

Cutting Strips and Squares

1. Press fabric.

2. Fold fabric in half, matching edges.

3. Lay fabric on cutting mat with most of it to the right. Line up left edges. Place ¼" line on 6" x 24" Ruler along left edge. Place hand on ruler to steady it with the little finger off the ruler's edge.

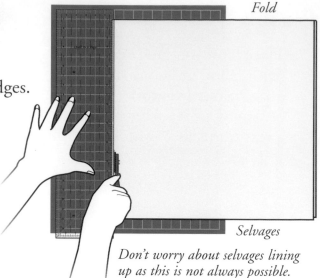

Fold

Selvages

Don't worry about selvages lining up as this is not always possible.

4. Take a rotary cutter in your free hand, and open blade. Apply pressure on ruler and cutter, and straighten fabric edge. Keep blade next to ruler's edge.

5. Reposition ruler, lined up to desired strip width.

6. Cut as far as your hand reaches on the ruler, then stop. "Walk" your hand up the ruler to reposition it without moving the ruler. Complete your cut.

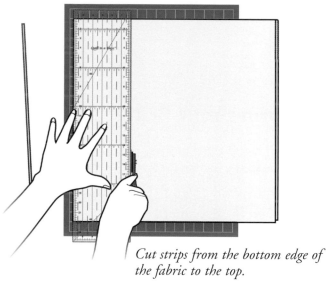

Cut strips from the bottom edge of the fabric to the top.

A "strip" refers to a selvage to selvage strip at least 42" long. A "half strip" refers to a strip at least 21" long.

7. Turn strip and square off selvage edges. Layer cut squares with 6", 9½", 12½", or 16" Square Up Ruler, depending on the size of square you need.

8. Repeat until you have the desired number of squares.

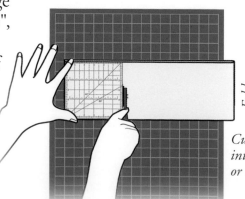

Fold

Cut strips into squares or rectangles.

Cutting with Shape Cut™ Plus

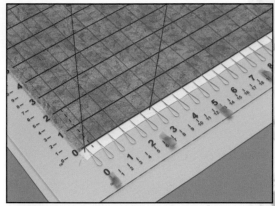

1. Use 18" Shape Cut™ Plus. Place Glow-Line™ tape at designated widths to avoid cutting errors.

2. Fold fabric into fourths, lining up selvage edges with fold. Smooth fabric flat.

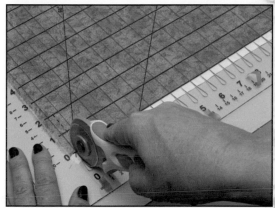

3. Place Shape Cut™ Plus on fabric. Line up zero horizontal line with bottom edge of fabric. Allow extra fabric to left of zero for straightening.

4. Place blade of cutter in zero line, and straighten left edge of fabric.

5. Cut strips at designated widths.

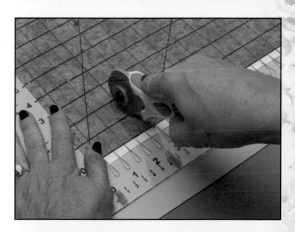

6. If strips are to be cut into squares, turn mat with strips on it. Square off selvage edges, and cut strips into desired sizes of squares.

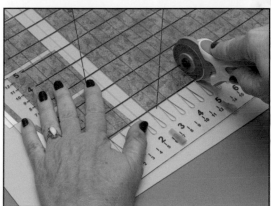

Fussy Cuts

A fussy cut is a selected image, such as a flower, centered on your patch. With a Fussy Cut Ruler™, you can cut the identical image repeatedly with ease.

There are three sizes of Fussy Cut Rulers™ available: 3½", 4½" and 6½". Perfect places for Fussy Cuts are the center or four corners of your block, or Cornerstones.

Pieced by Eleanor Burns
Quilted by Amie Potter
40" x 40"

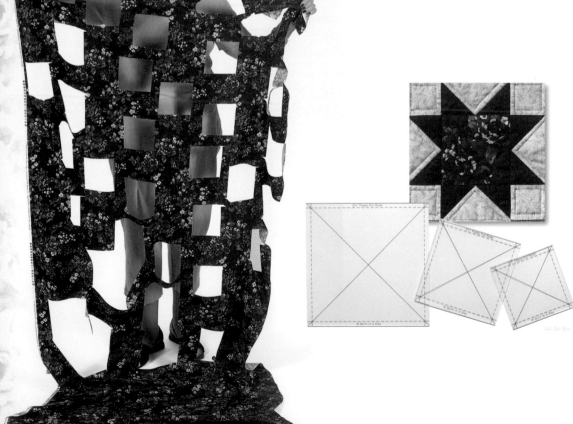

*Your remaining fabric looks like
"swiss cheese" after fussy cutting.*

How to Make a Fussy Cut

1. To keep ruler from slipping while cutting, cut InvisiGRIP™ ½" smaller than ruler and press on bottom side.

2. Find image on fabric that fits within size needed.

3. Place ruler on top of image, with center of X on center of image. The dashed lines indicate the seam lines. Shift ruler so image fits within seam lines.

4. If it's critical that each image be identical, place a piece of InvisiGRIP™ on top side of Fussy Cut Ruler. Trace outline of fussy cut on the top piece with a permanent marking pen. Remove top InvisiGRIP™ after cutting all your squares.

5. Cut around ruler with rotary cutter. To help with accuracy, place fabric on Brooklyn Revolver™ or Olfa Rotating Mat.

6. Move ruler to next fussy cut, line up ruler on image, and repeat.

7. To make your own template, cut appropriate size square from template plastic. Draw an X and ¼" seam lines. Place on image, draw around template, and cut out with rotary cutter and ruler.

Calculating Yardage for Stripes

Stripes can be used for Lattice or Borders. If there is a narrow stripe and a wide stripe in the same piece of fabric, use the narrow stripe for Lattice and the wide stripe for Borders.

1. Select a stripe with the same width recommended for your selected project.

2. Count the number of repeats in the stripe, and compare that number against the number of stripes needed.

3. If you are using the stripe for Lattice, refer to the length of your block row. Divide that number by 36" for stripe yardage.

4. If you are using the stripe for an outside Border, and will miter the corners, add 12" to the finished total length of your selected quilt. Divide that number by 36" for stripe yardage.

Cutting Stripes

1. Lay out end of stripe fabric selvage to selvage on a cutting mat. Plan which lines to cut.

2. With the 6" x 24" ruler, cut on the line the length of the ruler. Without moving fabric, move the ruler to the next line, and cut the length of the ruler. Continue to cut stripes the length of the ruler across the width of the fabric.

3. Pull the uncut fabric toward you, and let the cut stripes fall off the end of table. Continue to cut stripes length of ruler until all stripes have been cut in continuous lengths.

Many beautiful striped fabrics are available for Lattice and Borders with different variables as to the size of the quilt, number of stripes across the width of fabric, and width of individual stripes. This yardage is an estimate for your Borders.

Lap	2⅓ yds
Twin	3½ yds
Full/Queen	3½ yds
King	3½ yds

To be sure you have enough fabric, you should calculate your own yardage. In the striped fabric used for this example, there were four narrow stripes, which was enough for the four 74" long Lattice. Since there were only four Lattice, figure an additional 54" for top and bottom Lattice.

74" for four vertical Lattice
+ 54" for top and bottom Lattice

128" divided by 36" = 3.55
(round up to 3⅔ yds.)

Pieced by Teresa Varnes
Quilted by Janna Mitchell
64" x 93"

For the Border, the stripe fabric used had four wide stripes plus a slightly narrower fifth stripe that was used for a casing on the back. Take the estimated finished length of 93" and add 12" for mitering the stripe.

93" for Side Borders
+ 12" for Mitering stripe

105" divided by 36" = 2.91
(round up to 3 yds.)

Purchase the larger amount of yardage, in this case 3⅔ yds, to get both Lattice and Borders from the same piece of striped yardage.

Winter

My Crazy Valentine

With bits and pieces from her scrap box, Teresa pieced a "heart felt" wallhanging. She fussy cut a rose for the center, and added a crocheted doily, lace, and buttons for embellishment.

Lodgepole Pine Quilt

This quilt is embellished with rich red cardinals and hand embroidered pine branches. The trees are made of strips from various shades of green.

Morning Star Quilt

Eleanor achieved an up to date look for this traditional pattern using crisp white background, red stars, and green chains. While the red and green are traditional holiday colors, this quilt is a star no matter what the season! The feathered machine quilting in the wide border, star blocks in each corner, and a floral border combine to further enhance the beauty of this quilt.

My Crazy Valentine Quilt

This is the perfect project to use your treasured scraps of fabric, bits of antique lace, slightly damaged handkerchiefs, antique buttons, and ribbon roses. Plus, this Valentine is fun, made with paper piecing techniques!

My Crazy Valentine is such a small scale quilt that you can add embellishments without investing a lot of time. For a special Valentine, you can personalize with photo transfer and related family heirlooms.

Inspiration Piece - Fabric One

Family One - Fabrics Two and Three

Family Two - Fabrics Four and Five

Corner Square

Border Stripe

Background

Pieced by Teresa Varnes
Quilted by Amie Potter
16" x 40"

Pieced and quilted by Teresa Varnes
16" x 16"

Fabric Selection

1168-15

Inspiration Fabric One

Start with your inspiration piece of fabric, such as a flower, bird, or another image appropriate for the recipient of the Valentine.

Once you have selected your inspiration fabric, select fabrics in two different color families and in different scales and textures.

1164-10

Family One
Fabric Two

1172-44

Family Two
Fabric Four

1166-10

Fabric Three

1167-49

Fabric Five

1166 15

Background

Select a medium or large scale fabric that coordinates with other fabrics and contrasts with the doily. For less distraction, the print could be tone on tone.

1171-10

Lattice

Select a stripe fabric approximately 3½" wide.

1167-49

Corner Squares

Select a fabric that contrasts with the Lattice in a different scale, or possible a fussy cut fabric for 3½" square.

Non-Woven Fusible Interfacing

Select non-woven light to medium weight fusible interfacing. One side of the interfacing is smooth in texture, while the other side has fusible dots. Fusible interfacing is used to turn under raw edges of applique. Do not confuse this interfacing with paper backed webbed fusing.

Supplies

Permanent Marking Pen
6½" Fussy Cut Ruler
12½" Square Up Ruler
#16 Needle on Sewing Machine to perforate paper

Light Table
A light table is useful, but a substitute is a light placed under an acrylic sewing table, or hold fabric up to light from window or lamp.

Embellish your Crazy Quilt with treasures such as silk ribbon roses, antique buttons, and lace. Add beads and pearls for sparkle! Select memorabilia in different scale and textures. In addition to cotton, look for heirloom satin and velvet, such as a small piece from a wedding dress.

If you like to hand embroider, use pearl cotton Size 8. Refer to your favorite hand embroidery instructions.

As an alternative, sew beautiful open machine embroidery stitches with silk ribbon in your bobbin.

Select an 8" Battenberg Heart Doily or 8" Crochet Lace Doily available in white or ecru.

Embellish with ⅜" - ⅝" wide lace or rickrack.

Yardage for Wallhangings

Finished Block Size 9½"

		One Valentine 16" x 16" One Heart Block	**Three Valentines** 16" x 40" Three Heart Blocks
Inspiration Piece	Fabric 1	**Five Different** **Fat Quarters or Stash** (1) 6½" square Fussy Cut Image should be 2" x 3"	**Five Different** **Fat Quarters or Stash** (3) 6½" squares Fussy Cut Image should be 2" x 3"
Family One	Fabric 2 Fabric 3	(1) 6" x 7" (1) 4" x 5½"	(3) 6" x 7" (3) 4" x 5½"
Family Two	Fabric 4 Fabric 5	(1) 4" x 7" (1) 5" x 9"	(3) 4" x 7" (3) 5" x 9"
Background		⅓ yd or Fat Quarter (1) 10" square	⅓ yd (3) 10" squares
Corner Squares or Fussy Cuts		⅛ yd (4) 3½" squares	⅛ yd (8) 3½" squares
Borders		⅛ yd (4) 3½" x 10"	⅓ yd (10) 3½" x 10"
or Border Stripe		⅓ yd Cut (4) 3½" x 10" strips lengthwise	⅔ yd Cut (10) 3½" x 10" strips lengthwise
Non-Woven Fusible Interfacing		¼ yd (1) 8" square	½ yd (3) 8" squares
Binding		¼ yd (2) 2¾" strips	⅓ yd (3) 2¾" strips
Backing		½ yd	½ yd
Batting	 100% Cotton	20" square (1) 7" square	20" x 44" (3) 7" squares

Sewing Crazy Quilt Pieces

1. Lay out fabrics.

2. Stack fabrics in numbered order.

3. Find pattern on Pattern Sheet and make a copy. Trim away excess paper so pattern is 8" square.

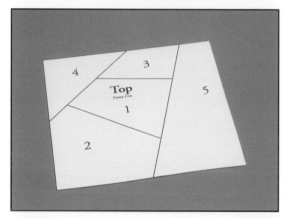

4. With printed side up, hold paper pattern up to light or window.

5. Center Fabric #1 Fussy Cut with **wrong side** of fabric against **plain side** of paper. Make sure design is placed with top up, and covering #1 paper patch. Pin in place.

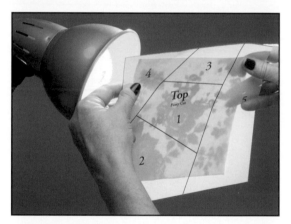

6. Turn to fabric side. Fold back paper and fabric and crease on printed line between #1 and #2.

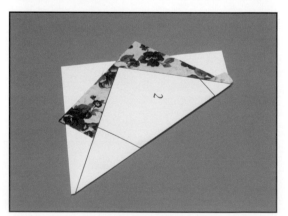

7. Open back up.

8. Place Fabric #2 with wrong side of fabric against plain side of paper. Hold up to light to make sure fabric covers #2 paper patch.

9. Flip #2 right sides together to #1. Slide #2 past crease for a ¼" seam. Pin.

10. Place open toe foot on sewing machine.

11. From printed side of paper, sew **on line** between #1 and #2 with small stitch length of 20 stitches per inch or 1.8 to 1.5 on computerized machines. Pull out pins.

    Do not sew past ends of line.

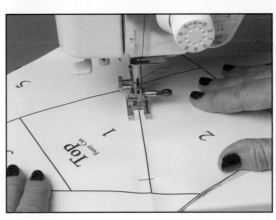

12. Fold paper back out of way. Trim seam to ¼".

13. From right side of fabric, finger-press seam between #1 and #2. Make sure #2 fabric covers #2 paper patch.

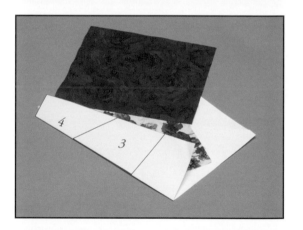

14. Fold back paper and fabric and crease on line between #3 and #1. Open.

15. From fabric side, flip #3 right sides together to #1. Slide fabric past crease for a ¼" seam. Pin.

16. From printed side of paper, sew on line between #1 and #3.

    Sew only on line. Do not sew past ends of line.

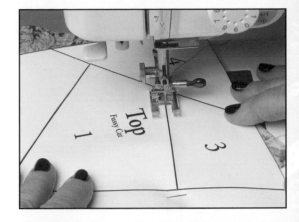

17. Fold paper back out of way. Trim seam to ¼". Fingerpress seam between #1 and #3 from fabric side.

18. **Optional:**
    From paper side, place pins on ends of lines #1/2 and #1/3 to mark intersection.

    From fabric side, sew narrow lace or ribbon on seam lines, or machine embroider decorative stitches. **Do not sew past pins.**

    See next page for Silk Ribbon by Machine.

Silk Ribbon Embroidery by Machine

1. As an alternative to decorative stitches, sew silk embroidery on lines by machine. Wind 4mm pure silk ribbon on bobbin.

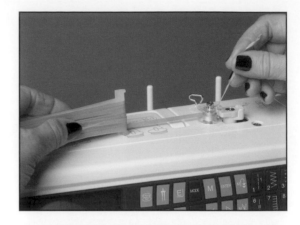

2. Place silk ribbon in the bobbin case, but not through the catch. Place matching thread on top.

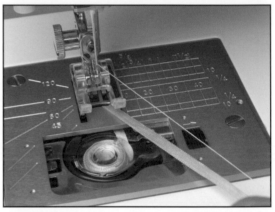

3. Choose big, wide open stitches as a feather or zig-zag. Sew on lines from paper side.

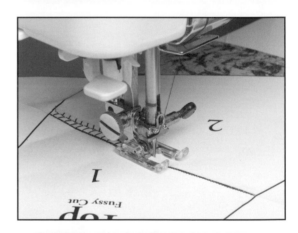

4. Turn over to see silk ribbon stitches on fabric side.

Finishing Crazy Quilt Pieces

1. Fold paper back, add #4, and trim.

2. Fold paper back, add #5, and trim. If necessary, tear paper away to trim seam.

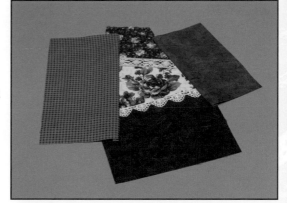

3. Trim excess fabric, following paper pattern.

4. Hold onto fabric and carefully pull away paper.

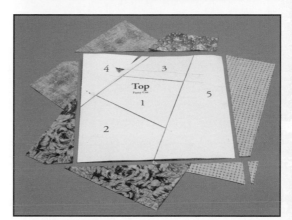

5. **Optional:** Embellish remaining seams with lace, or decorative stitches **by machine.**

6. If you plan to **hand embroider,** embroider seams **after** Heart is backed with fusible interfacing and turned.

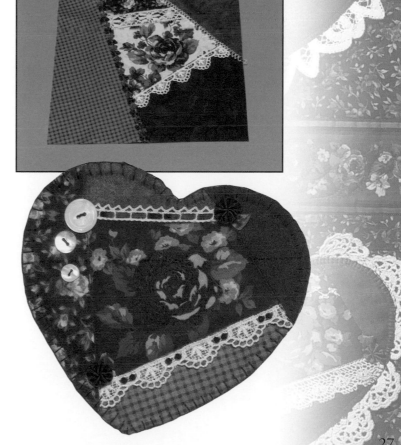

Making Heart for 8" Doily

1. Fold an 8½" x 11" piece of paper in half.

2. Photo copy doily, or put doily on light table or window. Line up fold on paper with center of Heart on doily. Using doily as a guide, trace Heart outline. Do not include lacy outside edge.

3. Cut out Heart pattern on folded paper. As an option, select large Heart pattern on Pattern Sheet to be used without doily.

4. Center Heart pattern on smooth side of 8" square fusible interfacing, and trace around pattern with permanent marking pen. Rough cut around heart, leaving about ½" outside the marked line.

5. Center fusible interfacing Heart on Crazy Quilt. Place bumpy, fusible side of interfacing against right side of fabric. Move interfacing to find interesting placement on patchwork. Pin.

6. Sew on lines with 1.8 or 20 stitches per inch.

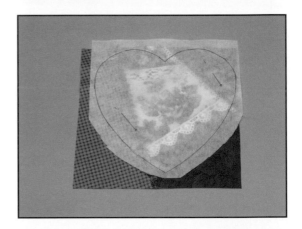

7. Trim ⅛" from lines. Clip in V of Heart.

8. Clip small hole in center of interfacing, and turn right side out.

9. Round out edges and press with little wooden iron or finger.

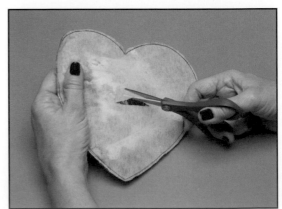

10. Do hand embroidery stitches on seam lines if desired.

11. Cut Heart shape from 100% cotton batting, and insert in Heart through opening with hemostat.

    If you hand embroidered through the interfacing, cut a slit in each section, and "pad" with a piece of cotton batting cut the same size.

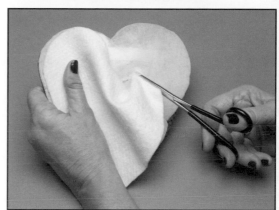

12. Machine stitch in the ditch through all thicknesses.

13. Center Crazy Quilt Heart on doily.

14. Steam press or pin Heart in place.

15. Fold 10" square Background in half, and press crease down center.

16. Center doily, and line up with crease. Pin, and topstitch doily in place around Heart.

17. Blanket stitch by hand or machine around outside edge of heart.

18. **Optional:** Sew rickrack around outside edge of Background square.

Adding Borders and Cornerstones

1. Measure length of Borders against size of Background. Trim Borders if necessary.

2. Lay out Hearts with Borders and Cornerstones.

3. Flip middle vertical row to left vertical row, right sides together.

4. Assembly-line sew.

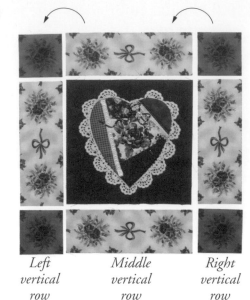

Left vertical row   *Middle vertical row*   *Right vertical row*

5. Flip right vertical row to middle vertical row, and assembly-line sew.

6. Sew remaining rows, pushing seams toward Borders and locking seams.

7. Layer Heart on batting and backing.

8. Stitch in the Ditch through seams, echo quilt around Heart, and bind.

9. Embellish as desired with buttons, silk ribbon roses, and memorabilia.

30

Pieced and quilted by Patricia Knoechel
16" x 16"

My Sisters are My Valentines

Patricia printed an old black and white photograph of her and her sisters on photo transfer fabric as the "heart" of her Valentine. The photo was taken some 50 years ago and is extra special because their mother, Erma Knoechel, made the girls' dresses for Easter Sunday. Notice how Patricia reversed the pattern to accommodate the shape of the photograph. She continues the nostalgia with her use of scraps of lace, rickrack, and tiny flower trim.

When Pigs Fly

Teresa took a whimsical approach to tease her Valentine. From novelty fabric, she fussy cut a flying pink pig. She used black background and a lacy white doily to give her Valentine a contemporary look. Quilting pattern found on Pattern Page.

Pieced and quilted by Teresa Varnes
16" x 16"

My Crazy Valentine

Sue was creative in her approach to this pattern. From a computer program "Vintage Prints," she selected a reproduction of an old Victorian Valentine and printed it on silk colorfast printer fabric. She embellished her Valentine with bits of lace, trim, and ribbon flowers.

Pieced and quilted by Sue Bouchard
16" x 16"

Lodgepole Pine Quilt

The Lodgepole Pine Quilt is repeated **Tree Blocks** on point, set together in diagonal rows and divided by Lattice and Cornerstones.

Set the theme from elegant to country with your fabrics. Fabrics with gold touches are perfect for elegant homes, and checks are great for homespun country decor.

Optional Cardinals add a refreshing new dimension, and offset the balance of the symmetrical trees. If you plan to sew Cardinals on your quilt, purchase Side and Corner Triangles, Lattice, and Borders in Background fabric. Eliminate a Folded Border. You can imagine the smell of pine needles with the addition of yarn stitches. Cardinal instructions begin on page 52.

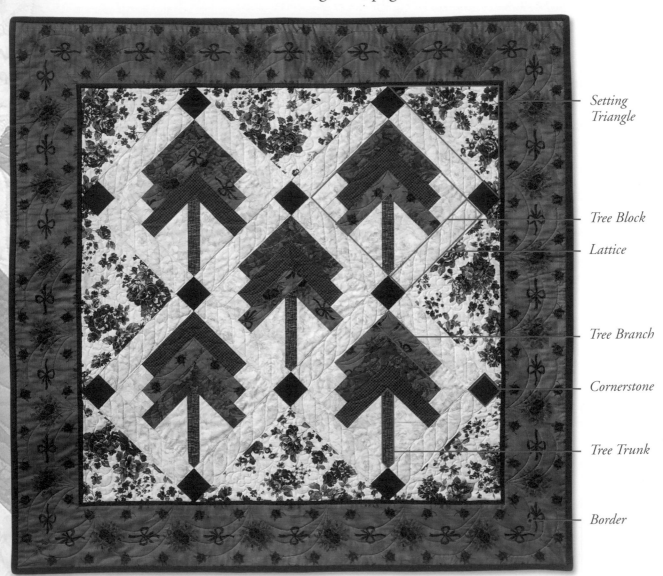

Setting Triangle

Tree Block

Lattice

Tree Branch

Cornerstone

Tree Trunk

Border

Pieced by Eleanor Burns
Quilted by Judy Jackson
Wallhanging 44" x 44"

Fabric Selection

1164-73

Background
Select a tone on tone in a range from light beige to a more woodsy light brown. A light check is charming for a country theme.

1169-49

1164-44

1167-49

Branches
Some trees in nature are blue green while others are more gray green or yellow green. Select all fabrics in one color tone, or mix a variety of greens into one quilt for richness and depth. Look for greens in slightly different values. Be brave in fabric selection! Trees made in similar values are boring. Choose from highly textured fabrics to tone on tone fabrics, checks, and patterns in different scales.

Trunk
Select brown fabric with an interesting texture in a low contrast pattern. For variety, use several different browns cut from your stash.

1168-10

Setting Triangles
Select a multi-colored large or small scale print that compliments the trees.

1164-73

Lattice
So that trees do not appear "crowded" with Lattice, purchase additional Background fabric, or another fabric in a similar value.

1172-10

Cornerstones
Pull an accent color from a multi-colored Border or the trees that adds a zing to the "forest."

1169-49

Borders
Select a large scale multi-colored print that pulls all colors together.

Supplies
6" Square Up Ruler
18" Shape Cut Plus™ Ruler
6" x 24" Ruler
4" x 14" Ruler
9½" Square Up Ruler

About the Block

The Lodgepole Pine is a strip pieced block made from three rows of branches, assembly-line sewn in order from bottom to top.

For a balanced look, it's important that matching 5" and 6½" Branches are sewn across from each other. In addition, trees are more interesting if the blocks are not all identical.

In this sample quilt, the center block looks lopsided because unmatched strips were sewn randomly. It could be disturbing to the eye.

Top Tree Branches

Middle Tree Branches

Bottom Tree Branches

Top Tree Branches
5" and 6½" strips with 3½" Background strips

Middle Tree Branches
5" and 6½" strips with 2" Background strips

Bottom Tree Branches
2" x 5" and 2" x 6½" strips

Scrappy Trees

If you want to make scrappy trees, use a variety of Background, greens, and browns from your stash, especially for Wallhanging and Lap. Follow your specific chart for amounts needed. Complete Yardage Charts are on pages 36-37.

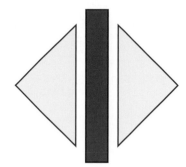

Trunks: Cut (1) 5" Background square and (1) 1½" x 8" brown for each Trunk.

Trees: Cut (1) 2" green strip at least 36" long into (3) 5" strips and (3) 6½" strips.

Bottom Branches: Set aside one set of 2" x 5" and 2" x 6½" strips for each tree.

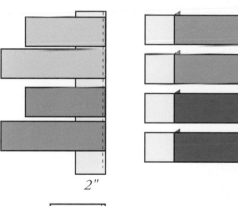

Middle Branches: Assembly-line sew matching 5" and 6½" strips to 2" Background strips. Cut apart, and press seams toward Branches.

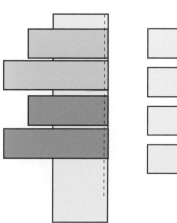

2"

Top Branches: Assembly-line sew matching 5" and 6½" strips to 3½" Background strips. Cut apart, and press seams toward Branches.

Block Assembly: Follow directions beginning on page 38.

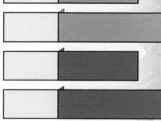

3½"

Lodgepole Pine Yardage Chart

Finished Block Size 9"

		Wallhanging 44" x 44" 5 Tree Blocks	Lap 50" x 66" 8 Tree Blocks
Background		⅔ yd	1 yd
	Trunk	(1) 5" strip cut into (5) 5" squares	(1) 5" strip cut into (8) 5" squares
	Top Branches	(1) 3½" strip cut into (6) 3½" x 7"	(1) 3½" strip cut into (6) 3½" x 7"
	Middle Branches	(1) 2" strip cut into (6) 2" x 7"	(1) 2" strip cut into (6) 2" x 7"
	Lattice	(4) 2½" strips cut later into (16) 2½" x size of block	(6) 2½" strips cut later into (24) 2½" x size of block
Branches		(3) different ¼ yds	(3) different ¼ yds
—		Cut each into (3) 6½" x 7" strips (3) 5" x 7" strips	Cut each into (3) 6½" x 7" strips (3) 5" x 7" strips
Trunk or Stash		⅛ yd (1) 1½" strip cut into (5) 1½" x 8"	¼ yd (2) 1½" strips cut into (8) 1½" x 8"
Cornerstones		¼ yd (1) 2½" strip cut into (12) 2½" squares	⅜ yd (2) 2½" strips cut into (17) 2½" squares
Folded Border		(4) 1¼" strips	(5) 1¼" strips
Setting Triangles		⅝ yd	1 yd
	Side Triangles Corner Triangles	(1) 17" square (2) 10½" squares	(2) 17" squares (2) 10½" squares
Borders	First Border	¾ yd (4) 6" strips	½ yd (5) 2½" strips
	Second Border	_____	1⅓ yds (6) 7½" strips
	Third Border	_____	_____
Binding		½ yd (5) 3" strips	⅝ yd (6) 3" strips
Backing		3 yds	4 yds
Batting		50" x 50"	56" x 72"

Twin	Full/Queen	King
76" x 108"	92" x 108"	108" x 108"
23 Tree Blocks	32 Tree Blocks	41 Tree Blocks

2⅛ yds	2¾ yds	3¾ yds
(3) 5" strips cut into	(4) 5" strips cut into	(6) 5" strips cut into
(23) 5" squares	(32) 5" squares	(41) 5" squares
(3) 3½" strips	(4) 3½" strips	(5) 3½" strips
Cut in half on fold	Cut in half on fold	Cut in half on fold
(3) 2" strips	(4) 2" strips	(5) 2" strips
Cut in half on fold	Cut in half on fold	Cut in half on fold
(15) 2½" strips cut later into	(20) 2½" strips cut later into	(25) 2½" strips cut later into
(60) 2½" x size of block	(80) 2½" x size of block	(100) 2½" x size of block
(9) different ¼ yds	(12) different ¼ yds	(15) different ¼ yds
Cut each into	Cut each into	Cut each into
(1) 6½" half strip	(1) 6½" half strip	(1) 6½" half strip
(1) 5" half strip	(1) 5" half strip	(1) 5" half strip
⅓ yd	⅜ yd	½ yd
(5) 1½" strips cut into	(7) 1½" strips cut into	(9) 1½" strips cut into
(23) 1½" x 8"	(32) 1½" x 8"	(41) 1½" x 8"
½ yd	⅔ yd	⅔ yd
(3) 2½" strips cut into	(4) 2½" strips cut into	(4) 2½" strips cut into
(38) 2½" squares	(49) 2½" squares	(60) 2½" squares
(7) 1¼" strips	(8) 1¼" strips	(9) 1¼" strips
1⅛ yds	1½ yds	1½ yds
(3) 17" squares	(4) 17" squares	(4) 17" squares
(2) 10½" squares	(2) 10½" squares	(2) 10½" squares
⅝ yd	⅔ yd	¾ yd
(7) 2½" strips	(8) 2½" strips	(9) 2½" strips
1½ yds	1½ yds	1¾ yds
(8) 5½" strips	(9) 5½" strips	(10) 5½" strips
2¼ yds	2¼ yds	2½ yds
(10) 7½" strips	(10) 7½" strips	(11) 7½" strips
1 yd	1 yd	1 yd
(10) 3" strips	(10) 3" strips	(11) 3" strips
6½ yds	8½ yds	10 yds
82" x 114"	98" x 114"	114" x 114"

Making Trunk

1. Cut 5" Background squares in half on one diagonal.

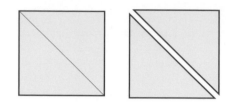

Number of 5" Squares	
Wallhanging	5
Lap	8
Twin	23
Full/Queen	32
King	41

2. Fold 1½" x 8" Trunk strips and Background triangles in half, and press folds.

3. Place Trunk strips with Background triangles. Line up crease with point on triangle, and sew with triangle on the bottom.

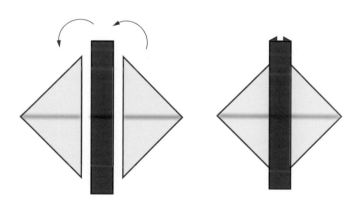

4. Press seams toward Trunk.

5. Square Trunks to 5" with 6" Square Up Ruler.

Center diagonal line on Trunk. Trim on right and top sides.

Turn patch. Do not turn ruler. Place ruler's 5" lines on freshly cut edges. Trim on right and top sides.

Cutting Bottom Branches of Tree

1. Stack **matching 5" and 6½"** Branch strips in the same order. Line up strips with lines on cutting mat.

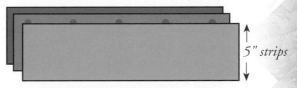

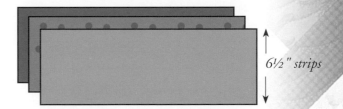

5" strips

6½" strips

Number of Strips

Wallhanging	(3) 7" long strips of each
Lap	(3) 7" long strips of each
Twin	3 half strips of each
Full/Queen	4 half strips of each
King	5 half strips of each

2. Straighten left end. Layer cut into 2" segments with Shape Cut™ Plus.

Number of 2" Segments

Wallhanging	5
Lap	8
Twin	23
Full/Queen	32
King	41

Cut strips for blocks every 2" with Shape Cut. See page 11.

3. As an alternative, use 4" x 14" ruler for cutting 2" pieces.

Optional: Cut extra fabric in 2" segments. Turn left overs into blocks and create your own pillows or tablerunner.

As an alternative, use 4" x 14" ruler and lines on cutting mat for cutting 2" pieces.

4. Place beside Trunk. Keep matching 5" and 6½" strips together.

5. Set aside.

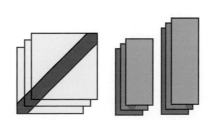

Sewing Middle Branches of Tree

1. Place 2" Background strips beside **matching 5" and 6½"** Branch strips stacked in the same order. Place cut edges at top.

Number of Strips

Wallhanging	(3) 7" long strips of each
Lap	(3) 7" long strips of each
Twin	3 half strips of each
Full/Queen	4 half strips of each
King	5 half strips of each

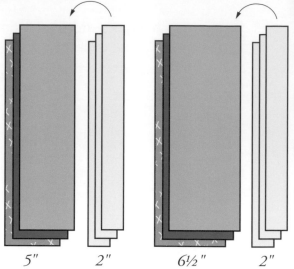

5"   2"   6½"   2"

2. Flip 2" Background strips right sides together to 5" and 6½" strips.

3. Assembly-line sew with ¼" seam.

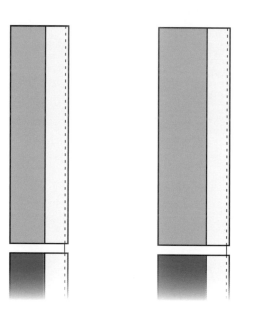

4. Set seams with Branch on top.

5. Open. Press seams toward Branch.

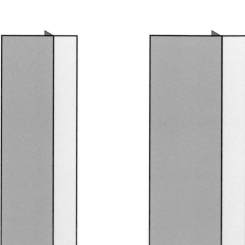

Cutting Middle Branches of Tree

1. Stack 5" and 6½" Branch strip sets on cutting mat. Line up with lines on cutting mat, staggering seams.

2. Straighten left end.

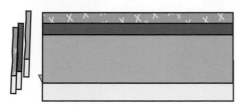 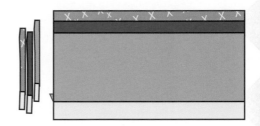

3. Layer cut strip sets into 2" segments. Cut one 5" and one 6½" for each Tree.

Number of 2" Segments	
Wallhanging	5
Lap	8
Twin	23
Full/Queen	32
King	41

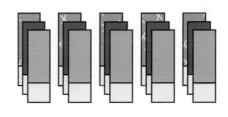

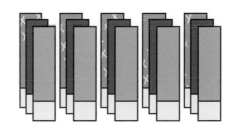

4. Place beside Trunk and Bottom Branches.

5. Set aside.

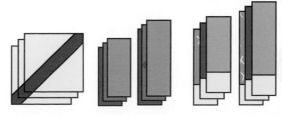

Sewing Top Branches of Tree

1. Place 3½" Background strips beside **matching 5" and 6½"** Branch strips. Place cut edges at top.

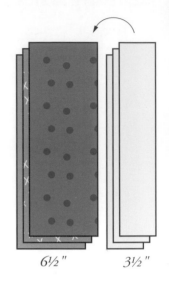
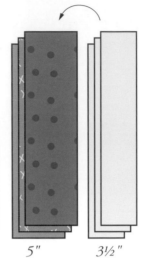

Number of Strips

Wallhanging	(3) 7" long strips of each
Lap	(3) 7" long strips of each
Twin	3 half strips of each
Full/Queen	4 half strips of each
King	5 half strips of each

5"   3½"   6½"   3½"

2. Flip 3½" Background strips right sides together to 5" and 6½" strips.

3. Assembly-line sew with ¼" seam.

4. Set seams with Branch on top. Open, and press seams toward Branch.

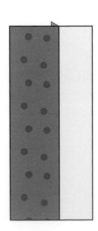
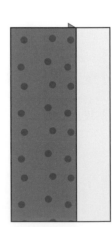

Cutting Top Branches of Tree

1. Stack **matching 5" and 6½"** Branch strip sets on cutting mat. Line up with lines on cutting mat, staggering seams.

2. Straighten left end.

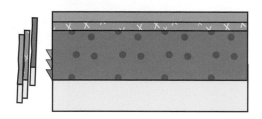

3. Layer cut strip sets into 2" segments.

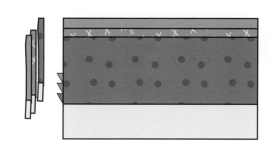

Number of 2" Segments	
Wallhanging	5
Lap	8
Twin	23
Full/Queen	32
King	41

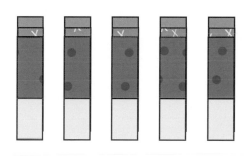

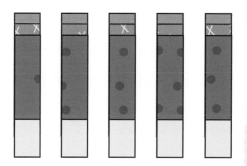

4. Place beside Trunk and other branches.

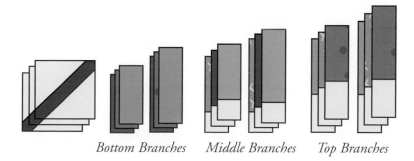

Bottom Branches   *Middle Branches*   *Top Branches*

Adding Bottom Branches to Trunk

Sew as illustrated so you don't "fight" seams.

1. Flip Trunk right sides together to 2" x 5" Branch.

2. Assembly-line sew. Clip apart.

3. Set seam with Branch on top, open, and press seam toward Branch.

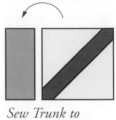

Sew Trunk to 2" x 5" Branch.

4. Flip 2" x 6½" Branch matching 2" x 5" strip right sides together to patch.

5. Assembly-line sew. Hold seams flat with stiletto. Clip apart.

6. Press seam toward Branch.

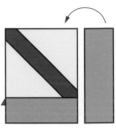

Sew 2" x 6½" Branch to Trunk

Adding Middle Branches

1. Flip patch right sides together to 5" Branch.

2. Assembly-line sew. Clip apart.

3. Press seam toward Middle Branch.

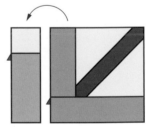

Flip patch right sides together to Branch.

4. Flip matching 6½" Branch right sides together to patch.

5. Assembly-line sew. Clip apart.

6. Press seam toward Middle Branch.

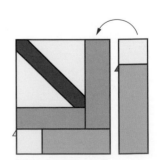

Flip 6½" Branch right sides together to patch.

Adding Top Branches

1. Flip patch right sides together to 5" Branch.

2. Assembly-line sew. Clip apart.

3. Press seam toward Top Branch.

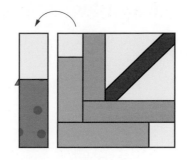

4. Flip matching 6½" Branch right sides together to patch.

5. Assembly-line sew. Clip apart.

6. Press seam toward Top Branch.

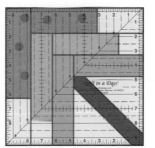

7. Measure several blocks to find average size. Size should be approximately 9½" square. Sliver trim to straighten if necessary.

   Your size _____

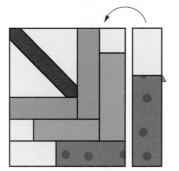

Place 9½" Square Up Ruler on block and measure.

Cutting Lattice and Cornerstones

1. Place 2½" Lattice strips on cutting mat. Trim selvage edges.

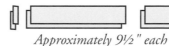

Approximately 9½" each   *Fold*

2. Layer cut into strips same size as block.

3. Cut 2½" strips for Cornerstones into 2½" squares.

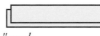

Number of	Blocks	Lattice	Cornerstones
Wallhanging	5	16	12
Lap	8	24	17
Twin	23	60	38
Full/Queen	32	80	49
King	41	100	60

Cutting Side and Corner Triangles

1. Cut 17" squares for Side Triangles on both diagonals.

Number of 17" Squares

Wallhanging	1
Lap	2
Twin	3
Full/Queen	4
King	4

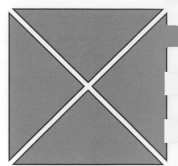

2. Cut two 10½" squares for Corners on one diagonal.

Lap, Twin, and Full/Queen Only:

1. Sew Cornerstone to Lattice, right sides together.

Number to Sew

Lap	1 for end of Row 3
Twin	2 for beginning and end of Row 4
Full/Queen	1 for end of Row 5

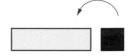

2. Press seam toward Lattice.

3. Sew Lattice/Cornerstone combination to Side Triangle.

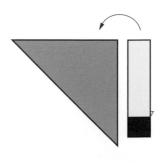

4. Press seam toward Lattice.

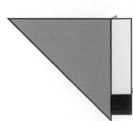

Sewing Top Together

1. Lay out your size quilt following layouts on next pages. Separate into rows.

2. Sew Lattice and Cornerstone rows together. Press seams toward Lattice.

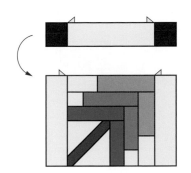

3. Sew Block and Lattice rows together. Press seams toward Lattice.

4. Sew Lattice/Cornerstone row and Lattice/Block row together. Press seams toward Lattice.

5. Place Side Triangles on ends of rows. Match 90° angles. Let tip on Triangles hang over.

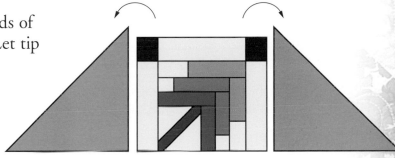

6. Sew with Triangles on bottom so bias doesn't stretch.

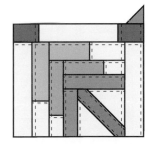

7. Press seams toward Lattice.

8. Trim tips from Triangles.

9. Sew rows together, matching Cornerstone and Lattice seams.

10. Press seams away from center.

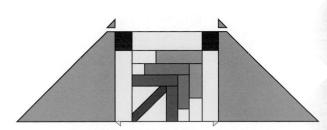

Twin

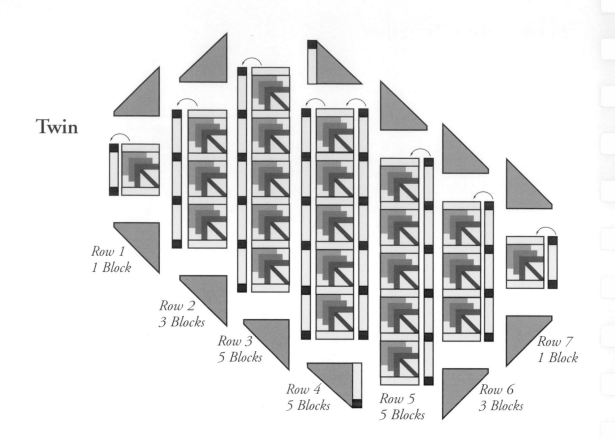

Row 1
1 Block

Row 2
3 Blocks

Row 3
5 Blocks

Row 4
5 Blocks

Row 5
5 Blocks

Row 6
3 Blocks

Row 7
1 Block

Full/Queen

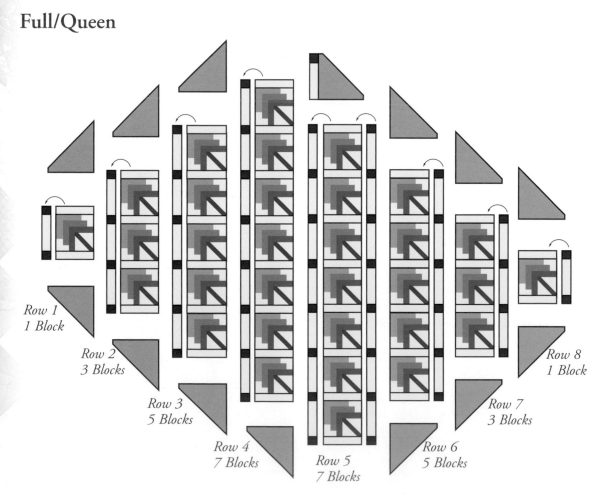

Row 1
1 Block

Row 2
3 Blocks

Row 3
5 Blocks

Row 4
7 Blocks

Row 5
7 Blocks

Row 6
5 Blocks

Row 7
3 Blocks

Row 8
1 Block

Wallhanging

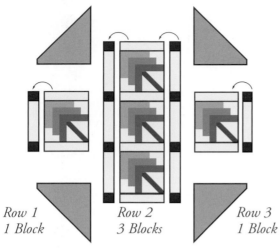

Row 1
1 Block

Row 2
3 Blocks

Row 3
1 Block

Lap

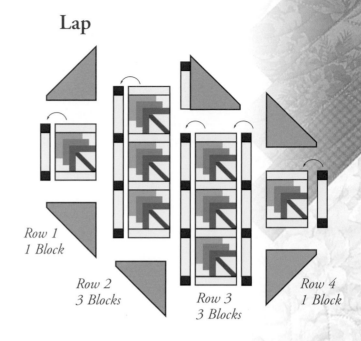

Row 1
1 Block

Row 2
3 Blocks

Row 3
3 Blocks

Row 4
1 Block

King

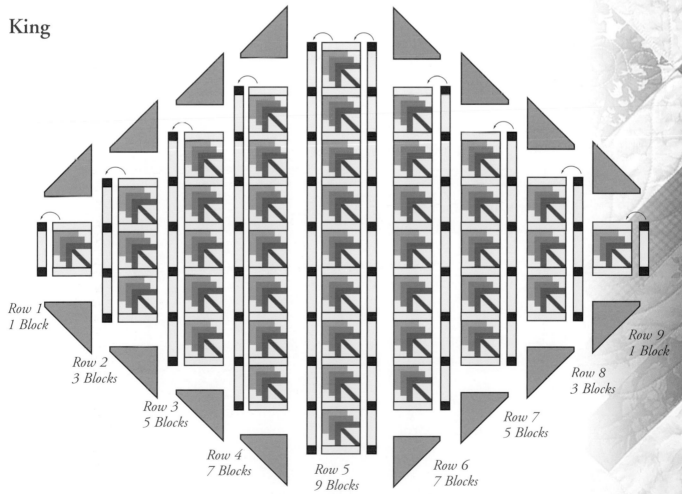

Row 1
1 Block

Row 2
3 Blocks

Row 3
5 Blocks

Row 4
7 Blocks

Row 5
9 Blocks

Row 6
7 Blocks

Row 7
5 Blocks

Row 8
3 Blocks

Row 9
1 Block

Adding Corners

1. Fold Corner triangles in half, and crease on fold.

2. Fold corners of top in half, and crease.

3. Match centers of Corners to centers of top. Pin, and sew with triangles on bottom.

4. Press seams toward Corners.

Squaring Outside Edges

1. Press top from wrong side and right side.

2. Lay top flat on cutting area.

3. Square outside edges, leaving ½" seam allowance for Folded Border.

• Place Quilt in a Day's 16" Square Up Ruler in upper right corner.

• Place ruler's ½" marks on points.

• Line up diagonal line on ruler with center of block.

• Trim two sides.

• Trim remaining corners.

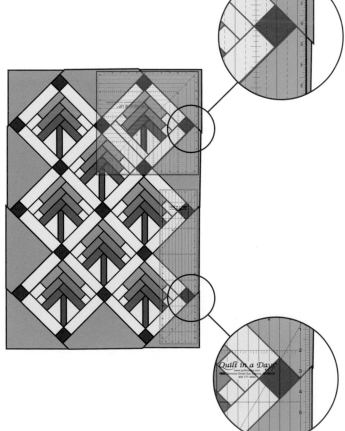

4. Line up 6" x 24" Ruler, and trim between Corners.

Adding Folded Border

1. If sides of quilt are longer than 1¼"
   Folded Border strips, piece Folded
   Border strips together.

2. Press 1¼" strips in half lengthwise,
   wrong sides together.

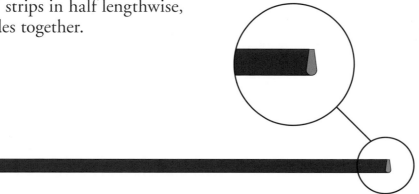

3. Place Folded Border on
   two opposite sides, matching
   raw edges.

4. Sew ⅛" seam from raw
   edges with 10 stitches per
   inch or 3.0 on computerized
   machines. Trim even with
   sides of quilt top.
   Do not fold out.

5. Repeat on remaining two
   sides, overlapping at corners.

6. Turn to **Adding Borders** on
   page 230.

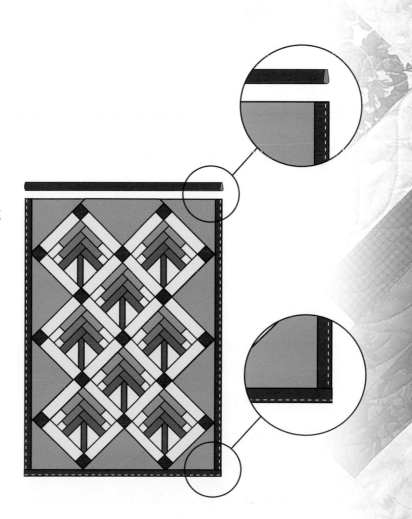

Making Optional Red Cardinals

Multiply these pieces by the total number of Cardinals desired for your quilt. For example, Lap has four Cardinals.

Red Body
    (1) 6" x 10"

1164-10

Darker Red Wing
    (1) 3" x 6"

1172-10

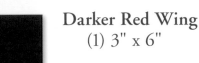

Non-woven Fusible Interfacing
    (1) 6" x 10"
    (1) 3" x 6"

100% Cotton Batting
    (1) 5" x 10"

Eye
    (1) Small black bead
Yarn
    Thin textured
    Brown and Green
Berries
    (6) Small red beads

Supplies
Large Eyed Needle
Permanent Marking Pen
Fat Drinking Straw
Ball Point Bodkin
Wooden Iron
Hemostat

Cardinals
Choose two values of red fabrics in different textures for Body and Wing. For other species of birds, round off the head, and change colors.

Fusible Interfacing
Select non-woven light to medium weight fusible interfacing. One side of the interfacing is smooth in texture, while the other side has fusible dots. Do not confuse this interfacing with paper backed webbed fusing. Fusible interfacing is used to turn under raw edges of Cardinal.

Cardinals in the Fall

Pieced by Eleanor Burns
Applique by Aiko Rogers
Quilted by Amie Potter
43" x 43"

Making Cardinals

1. Find Cardinal patterns on Pattern Sheet. Trace Cardinal patterns on template plastic, and cut out.

 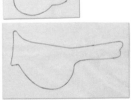

2. Turn interfacing with smooth side up. Trace around templates with fine point permanent marking pen. Turn templates over and trace pieces for right side of quilt.

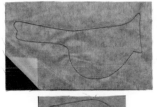

Trace templates for Cardinal on left side of quilt. Wallhanging and Lap have three Cardinals facing right.

Turn templates over and trace pieces for right side of quilt. Wallhanging and Lap have one Cardinal facing left.

3. Trace as many Cardinals as desired for your size quilt.

4. Place rough, fusible side of interfacing against right side of corresponding fabric. Pin.

5. With 20 stitches per inch or 1.5 on computerized machines, sew on drawn lines.

6. Trim seams to ⅛". Clip to stitching inside curves.

7. Cut a small opening in center of interfacing on each piece.

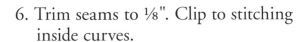

8. Insert straw into hole. Push straw against fabric.

9. Place ball of bodkin **on fabric** stretched over straw, and gently push fabric into straw about 1½" with bodkin. Remove straw and bodkin.

10. Insert straw and bodkin in second half about 1", and finish turning right side out with your fingers. Run bodkin around inside edge and poke out.

11. From right side, pull out points with pin or stiletto.

12. Push fabric over interfacing edge with wooden iron.

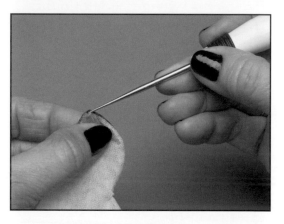

13. Cut 100% cotton batting same size as piece. Insert batting through opening with hemostat.

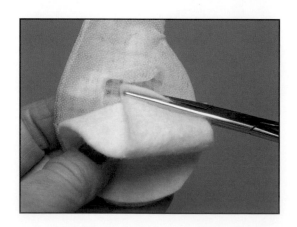

Sewing Cardinals and Pine Needles

1. Lay out quilt top, and plan placement of Cardinals on Side Triangles, extending into Border.

2. Pin Cardinals in place.

3. **Pine Needle Stencil:** Make a photo copy of pattern found on Pattern Sheet.

4. With sharp scissors, cut on lines to make slits for your pencil.

5. Place paper stencil under Cardinal on left side of quilt, and trace branch lines with pencil. On opposite side of quilt, turn stencil upside down and trace reverse image.

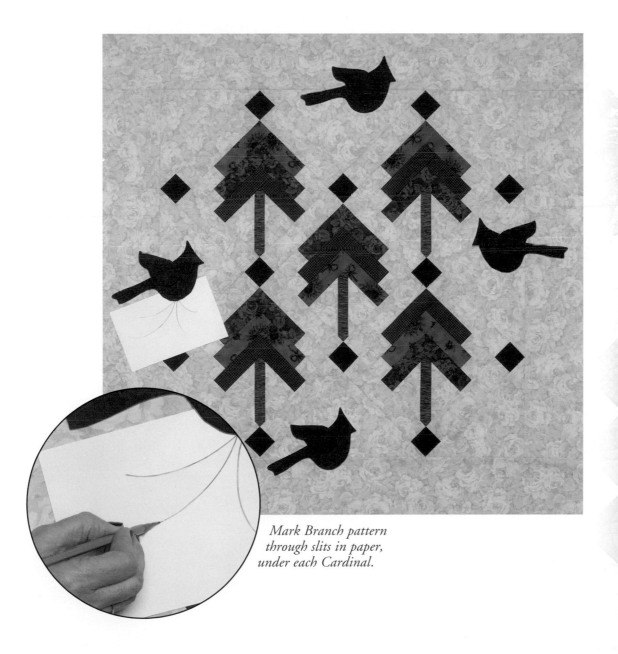

Mark Branch pattern through slits in paper, under each Cardinal.

6. Backstitch on branch lines with brown yarn. Come up through A, back down through B, and out again through C. Repeat process.

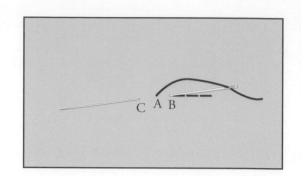

7. Ladder stitch pine needles with green yarn.

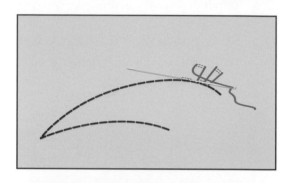

8. Steam press body of Cardinal in place. Steam press Wing in place. Press from wrong side.

9. Blanket stitch outside edge of Cardinal by hand or machine.

10. Sew on bead eye, and optional red beads.

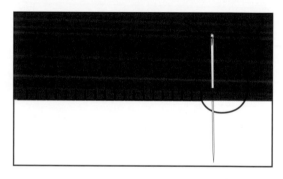

11. Turn to **Layering Your Quilt** on page 231.

Lodgepole pine forests provide shelter for deer, elk, moose, and bears. For her Wallhanging below, Irene found bears cut from picture fabric was not only a playful addition to her woodsy quilt, but they helped hide some not so straight trunks!

If your trunks aren't perfectly straight, don't fret. The scientific name *Pinus contorta* means "twisted pine."

Bear detail

Pieced by Irene Ashkenas
Quilted by Phyllis Strickland
38" x 38"

Lodgepole pine forests provided logs for this mountain home belonging to Eleanor Burns in Julian, California.

Fall Foliage

Enjoy making smaller 6" finished size Tree Blocks. To showcase your favorite fall fabrics, use the same fabric in each tree.

Pieced by Sue Bouchard
Quilted by Amie Potter
32" x 42"

1. Make the Trunk with 4" Background squares and 1¼" x 5½" Trunk fabric. Follow instructions on page 38, and square up to 3½".

2. Assembly-line sew Branches following illustration on right. Sew one set for each tree.

3. Sew blocks together following illustrations on pages 44 and 45.

4. For putting your quilt together, follow Lap instructions.

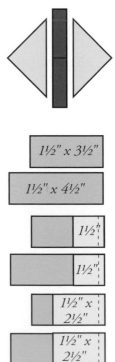

1½" x 3½"

1½" x 4½"

1½"

1½"

1½" x 2½"

1½" x 2½"

Fall Foliage Yardage Chart

Finished Block Size 6"

32" x 42"

8 Tree Blocks

Background	¼ yd
Trunk	(1) 4" strip cut into
	(8) 4" squares
Branches	(2) 1½" strips cut into
Middle Branches	(16) 1½" x 1½"
Top Branches	(16) 1½" x 2½"
Lattice	¼ yd
	(4) 1½" strips cut into
	(24) 1½" x 6½"
Branches	⅛ yd of Eight Different Colors
	(1) 1½" strip from each cut into
	(3) 1½" x 3½"
	(3) 1½" x 4½"
Trunk	⅛ yd
	(2) 1¼" strips cut into
	(8) 1¼" x 5½"
Cornerstones	⅛ yd
	(1) 1½" strip cut into
	(17) 1½" squares
Setting Triangles	⅜ yd
Side Triangles	(2) 11½" squares
	Cut on both diagonals
Corner Triangles	(2) 7" squares
	Cut on one diagonal
Borders	¼ yd
First Border	(4) 1½" strips
Second Border	⅝ yd
	(4) 4½" strips
Binding	⅓ yd
	(4) 2¾" strips
Backing	1¼ yds
Batting	40" x 50"

Morning Star Quilt

There are three pieced units that go into the Morning Star Quilt: the **Chain Block, Border Chain Rectangle, and Star Block.**

The Chain Block and Border Chain Rectangle are made at the same time from strips. The points in the Star are made with 2" x 4" finished size Flying Geese patches.

Two other pieces are cut from Background fabric: Border Rectangles and Corners. Plain Borders finish the Wallhanging and Lap. Additional Star blocks finish off corners on the Second Border for Twin, Full/Queen, and King. Yardage for these four Stars are included in the charts.

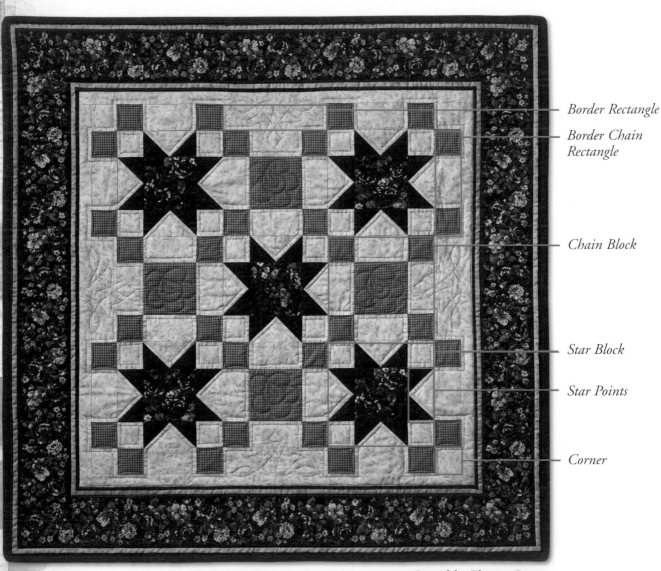

Border Rectangle

Border Chain Rectangle

Chain Block

Star Block

Star Points

Corner

Pieced by Eleanor Burns
Quilted by Amie Potter
40" x 40"

Fabric Selection

1171-10

Inspiration Piece
Begin by selecting a multi-colored inspiration fabric. This could become the Chain, Star Center, or Border. From that fabric, select at least two color families. The Star should be the darker of the two, with the Chain being the medium.

1172-73

Background
Select a small to large scale tone on tone that matches Backgrounds of the other fabrics, yet contrasts with the two color families.

1167-49

Chain
Select one large scale, multi-colored fabric. This block is also perfect for scrappy, multiple fabrics. If you want to make it scrappy, use a different fabric for each strip. This fabric could also be the Second Border in the Wallhanging, Lap, and the Third Border in Twin, Full/Queen and King sizes.

1164-10

Star Points
Select a large scale tone on tone that reads solid from a distance. If you use a multi-colored fabric, points are sometimes lost to a light part of the fabric. Consider selecting this fabric for the First Border as well because it frames the top beautifully.

1168-15

Star Center
Select a fabric that coordinates with the Star Points. It could be your inspiration piece. This 4½" square is also perfect for a fussy cut. To figure yardage, count out the same number of 4½" squares on your fabric as is needed for Stars in your size quilt.

Supplies

6" x 12" Ruler
4½" Fussy Cut Ruler
4" x 8" Large Flying
    Geese Ruler

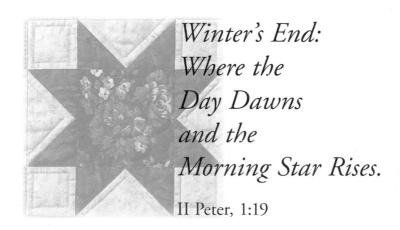

Winter's End: Where the Day Dawns and the Morning Star Rises.

II Peter, 1:19

Morning Star Yardage Chart

		Wallhanging 38" x 38" 3 x 3, 9 Blocks	Lap 56" x 72" 5 x 7, 35 Blocks
Finished Block Size 8"			
Background		⅔ yd	1¾ yds
	Chain Background	(1) 4½" strip (1) 2½" strip	(3) 4½" strips (5) 2½" strips
	Star Background	(1) 5½" strip cut into (5) 5½" squares	(3) 5½" strips cut into (18) 5½" squares
	Corners	(2) 2½" strips cut into (24) 2½" squares	(5) 2½" strips cut into (76) 2½" squares
	Border Rectangles	(1) 2½" strip	(1) 2½" strip
Chain Blocks		4 Blocks	17 Blocks
		⅓ yd (2) 2½" strips (1) 4½" strip	1 yd (6) 2½" strips (3) 4½" strips
Star Blocks		5 Blocks	18 Blocks
	Star Points	¼ yd (1) 7" strip cut into (5) 7" squares	1 yd (4) 7" strips cut into (18) 7" squares
	Star Center or 4½" Fussy Cut	¼ yd (1) 4½" strip cut into (5) 4½" squares	½ yd (3) 4½" strips cut into (18) 4½" squares
First Border		¼ yd (4) 1½" strips	⅓ yd (6) 1½" strips
Second Border		¾ yd (4) 4½" strips	1⅓ yds (7) 6" strips
Third Border		——	——
Binding		½ yd (4) 3" strips	⅔ yd (7) 3" strips
Backing		1¼ yds	4½ yds
Batting		44" x 44"	62" x 78"

Twin	Queen	King
74" x 106"	90" x 106"	106" x 106"
5 x 9, 45 Blocks	7 x 9, 63 Blocks	9 x 9, 81 Blocks

Twin	Queen	King
2½ yds	3¼ yds	4 yds
(4) 4½" strips	(5) 4½" strips	(7) 4½" strips
(6) 2½" strips	(8) 2½" strips	(10) 2½" strips
(4) 5½" strips cut into	(6) 5½" strips cut into	(7) 5½" strips cut into
(27) 5½" squares	(36) 5½" squares	(45) 5½" squares
(7) 2½" strips cut into	(10) 2½" strips cut into	(12) 2½" strips cut into
(112) 2½" squares	(148) 2½" squares	(180) 2½" squares
(3) 2½" strips	(4) 2½" strips	(4) 2½" strips
22 Blocks	31 Blocks	40 Blocks
1⅛ yds	1½ yds	1⅔ yds
(8) 2½" strips	(10) 2½" strips	(13) 2½" strips
(3) 4½" strips	(4) 4½" strips	(5) 4½" strips
27 Blocks	36 Blocks	45 Blocks
1⅓ yds	1¾ yds	2 yds
(6) 7" strips cut into	(8) 7" strips cut into	(9) 7" strips cut into
(27) 7" squares	(36) 7" squares	(45) 7" squares
¾ yd	¾ yd	1 yd
(4) 4½" strips cut into	(5) 4½" strips cut into	(6) 4½" strips cut into
(27) 4½" squares	(36) 4½" squares	(45) 4½" squares
⅝ yd	⅝ yd	⅔ yd
(7) 2½" strips	(7) 2½" strips	(8) 2½" strips
2 yds	2⅛ yds	2⅛ yds
(7) 8½" strips	(8) 8½" strips	(8) 8½" strips
1⅝ yds	1⅞ yds	2 yds
(9) 6" strips	(10) 6" strips	(11) 6" strips
⅞ yd	1 yd	1 yd
(9) 3" strips	(10) 3" strips	(11) 3" strips
6½ yds	9½ yds	10 yds
80" x 112"	96" x 112"	112" x 112"

Making Chain Blocks and Chain Border Rectangles

Take the ¼" Seam Test so Chain Blocks and Star Blocks finish the same size. (See page 8.)

Making Section One

1. Place 4½" Background strips with two stacks of 2½" Chain strips.

Number of Strips in Each Stack	
Wallhanging	1 strip
Lap	3 strips
Twin	4 strips
Full/Queen	5 strips
King	6½ strips

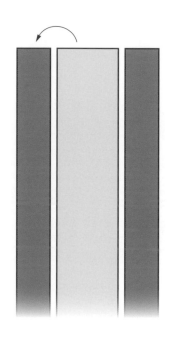

2. Sew 4½" Background strips to left 2½" Chain strips lengthwise with accurate ¼" seams.

*Follow pressing steps closely so seams on the finished
Chain Blocks lock with seams on finished Star Blocks.*

3. Place Section One on a
   pressing mat with 4½"
   Background on top.
   Set seam.

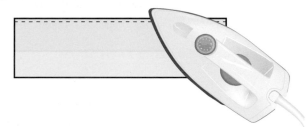

4. Open, and press seams
   to Background. Check
   width. Width should be
   approximately 6½".

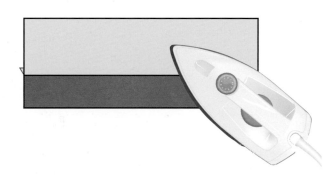

5. Sew second 2½" Chain
   strip, and press seams **to
   Background.**

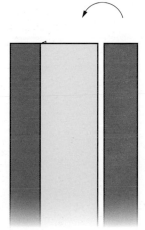

6. Place Section One on cutting mat. Square off left end.

7. Cut into 2½" sections with 4" x 14" Ruler, 6" x 12" Ruler, or Shape Cut.

Number of 2½" sections

Wallhanging	16
Lap	48
Twin	60
Full/Queen	80
King	100

Approximately 8½"

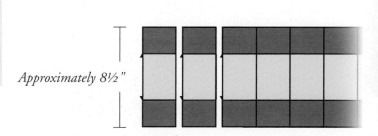

Making Section Two

1. Place 4½" Chain strip with two stacks of 2½" Background strips.

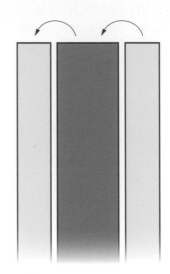

Number of Strips in Each Stack

Wallhanging	½ strip
Lap	2½ strips
Twin	3 strips
Full/Queen	4 strips
King	5 strips

2. Assembly-line sew strips.

3. Place on pressing mat with 2½" Background strips on top. Set seams.

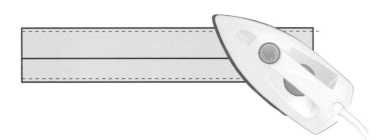

4. Open, and press **toward Background.**

5. Square off left end.

8½"

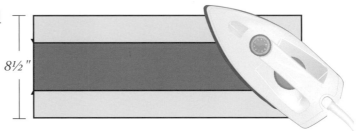

6. Cut into 4½" sections, and stack.

Number of 4½" Sections

Wallhanging	4
Lap	17
Twin	22
Full/Queen	31
King	40

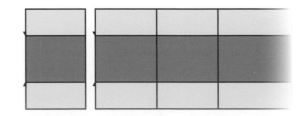

Sewing Chain Block Together

1. Lay out two stacks of Section One and one stack of Section Two.

Number in Each Stack	
Wallhanging	4
Lap	17
Twin	22
Full/Queen	31
King	40

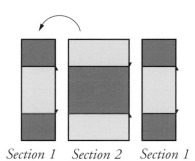

Section 1   Section 2   Section 1

2. Assembly-line sew Section Two to Section One, matching seams. Push the seams in the same direction they were pressed.

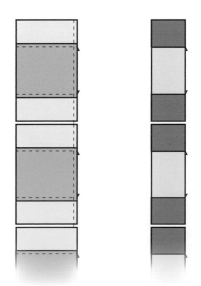

3. Sew second stack of Section One.

4. Cut apart.

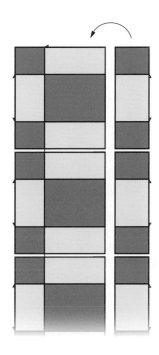

5. Place Chain Block wrong side up on pressing mat. Press just sewn seams **toward center.**

6. Measure. Block should be approximately 8½" square.

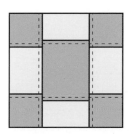

Press just sewn seams toward center.

✉ Making Star Points

1. Place smaller 5½" Background square right sides together and centered on larger 7" Star Point square.

Count out this many of each square	
Wallhanging	5
Lap	18
Twin	27
Full/Queen	36
King	45

2. Place 6" x 12" Ruler on squares so ruler touches all four corners. Draw diagonal line across squares. Pin.

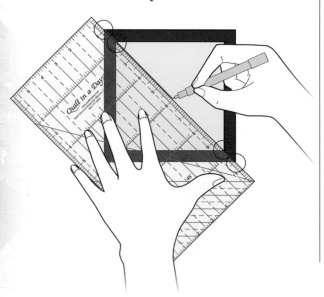

3. Sew **exactly** ¼" from both sides of drawn line. Use 15 stitches per inch or 2.0 on computerized machines. Assembly-line sew squares. Press to set seam.

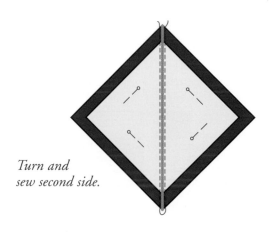

Turn and sew second side.

4. Remove pins. Cut on drawn line.

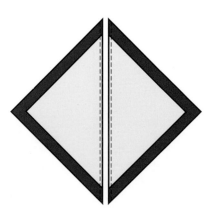

5. Place on pressing mat with large triangle on top. Press to set seam.

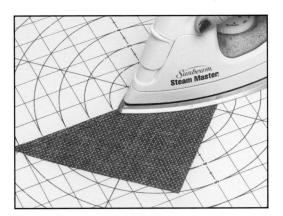

6. Open and press flat. Check that there are no tucks, and seam is pressed toward larger triangle.

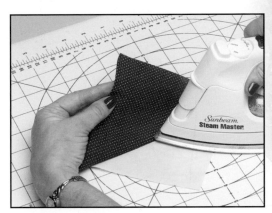

7. Place pieces right sides together so that opposite fabrics touch with Star Points matched to Background. Seams are parallel with each other.

Seams are pressed toward larger triangle.

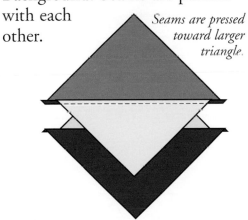

8. Match up outside edges. Notice that there is a gap between seams. **The seams do not match.**

Match outside edges.

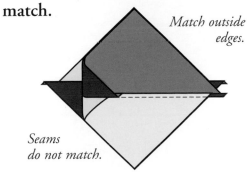

Seams do not match.

9. Draw a diagonal line across seams. Pin. Sew ¼" from both sides of drawn line. Hold seams flat with stiletto so seams do not flip. Press to set seam.

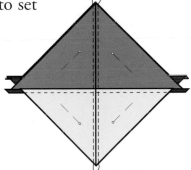

10. Cut on the drawn line.

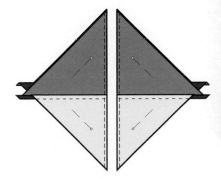

11. Fold in half and clip to the stitching. This allows the seam allowance to be pressed away from Background.

12. From right side, press into one Background. Turn and press into second Background.

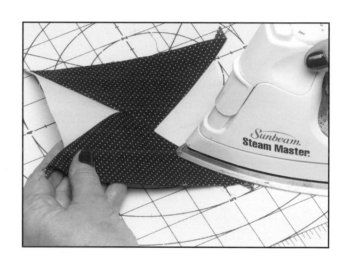

13. Turn over, and press on wrong side. At clipped seam, fabric is pressed away from Background.

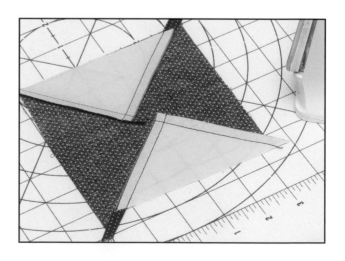

2½" x 4½" Patches Finished at 2" x 4"

Squaring Up with Large Geese Ruler

1. Line up Large Geese Ruler's red lines on 45° sewn lines. Line up dotted line with peak of triangle for ¼" seam allowance. Cut block in half to separate two patches.

Use Large Geese Ruler. Place 2" x 4" finished Geese red lines on seam.

2. Trim off excess fabric on right. Hold ruler securely on fabric so it does not shift while cutting.

Cut in half. Trim on right.

3. Turn patch around. **Do not turn ruler.** Line up red straight line with trimmed bottom edge. Line up green diagonal line with seam.

4. Trim off excess fabric on right and top.

5. Repeat with second half.

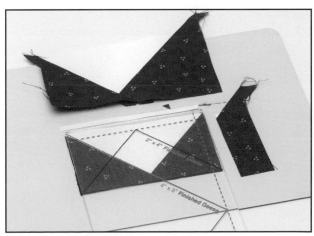

Trim to 2½" x 4½".

Making Stars

1. Lay out the 4½" Center Square, 2½" Corner Squares, and Star Points. Stack pieces for assembly-line sewing.

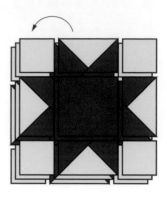

Make this many Stars	
Wallhanging	5
Lap	18
Twin	27
Full/Queen	36
King	45

2. Flip middle row to left. Assembly-line sew all vertical seams. Clip apart after every third patch.

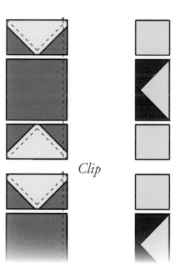

Clip

3. Open and assembly-line sew right row. Clip apart after every third patch.

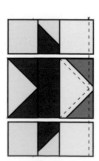

4. Turn. Sew right row, pressing seams toward Star Center, and away from Star Points. Lock seams.

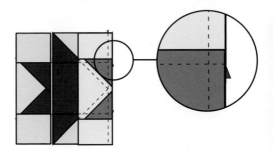

5. Sew second row, repeating seams. Set seams, open, and press seams away from center.

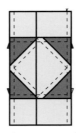

6. Check from wrong side. Just sewn seams should be pressed away from center.

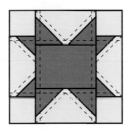

Cutting Plain Border Rectangles

1. Measure your block. It should be approximately 8½" square, the same size as the Chain Block.

2. Cut 2½" Background strips into Border Rectangles the same size as your blocks.

3. Cut four 2½" Background Corners for each quilt.

Number of Border Rectangles	
Wallhanging	4
Lap	10
Twin	12
Full/Queen	14
King	16

Sewing Blocks Together

1. Lay out your selected size quilt in a large area following the corresponding illustration.

   Alternate between the Star Block and the Chain Block, beginning and ending with Star Blocks in the corners. Begin each row with the opposite of block above it.

2. Place Chain Border Rectangles beside all Star Blocks around outside edge to continue Chain.

Twin – 5 x 9

Queen – 7 x 9

3. Place Plain Border Rectangles beside all Chain Blocks around outside edge.

4. Place 2½" Background Corner Squares in all four corners.

5. Assembly-line sew vertical rows together. Do not clip connecting threads. Refer to **Sewing Top Together**, pages 114-115.

6. See **Pressing Horizontal Rows for Locking Seams** on page 76.

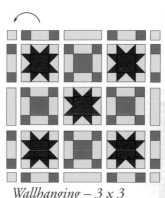

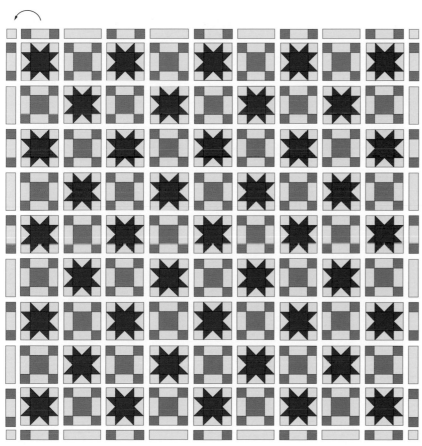

King – 9 x 9

Wallhanging – 3 x 3

Lap – 5 x 7

Pressing Horizontal Rows for Locking Seams

1. From the wrong side, press top and bottom horizontal rows as illustrated.

2. Press seams in middle rows away from Stars toward Chain Blocks.

3. Sew horizontal rows.

4. Press just sewn rows in one direction from wrong side. Press from right side.

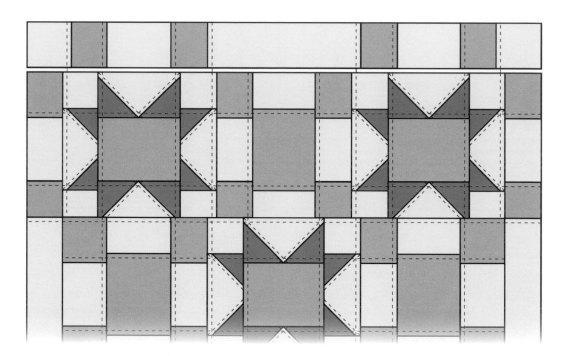

Adding Borders

1. Sew First Border to all sizes.

2. **Wallhanging and Lap:** Sew Second Border.

3. Turn to **Layering Your Quilt**, page 231.

Sewing Second Border with Star Corners

This Border treatment is for Twin, Full/Queen, and King only. If your Star blocks are different than 8½", cut your Second Border strips to that size.

1. Trim selvages on 8½" strips.

2. Piece strips together to fit two sides and top and bottom of quilt.

	Sides	Top and Bottom
Twin	2 strips each	1½ strips each
Full/Queen	2 strips each	2 strips each
King	2 strips each	2 strips each

3. Measure and cut two 8½" strips same length as sides.

4. Measure and cut two 8½" strips same length as top and bottom.

5. Pin and sew 8½" Borders to sides. Press seams toward Second Border.

6. Sew Stars to ends of top and bottom strips. Press seams toward Second Border.

7. Pin and sew to top and bottom. Press seams toward Second Border.

8. Sew Third Border.

9. Turn to **Layering Your Quilt**, page 231.

Spring

Twin Sisters

Sue's scrappy quilt is fresh and cheerful in springy blues and yellows with crisp white accents. A wide border stripe completes Sue's quilt, but you can also make a rainbow border.

Baskets and Bows

Blue baskets filled with pretty posies set the theme for Patty's wallhanging. In shades of blue and yellow, spring is in the air. The border stripe of bows and flowers frame the quilt beautifully.

Gone Fishing

Sue's colorful fish are sure to delight children of any age, as they swim by on a blue background that creates the perfect cool, clear water.

Gone Fishing Quilt

The **Fish Block** is made of two Little Fish units and one Big Fish unit, in three different color families. Finished size of block is 17" x 22".

Placement of the three units is interchangeable by sewing water spacers in front or back of Little Fish and on top or bottom of Big Fish. Each quilt can be made with a combination of blocks in these different layouts from Wallhanging to Full/Queen.

Fish can "swim" in opposite directions as well.

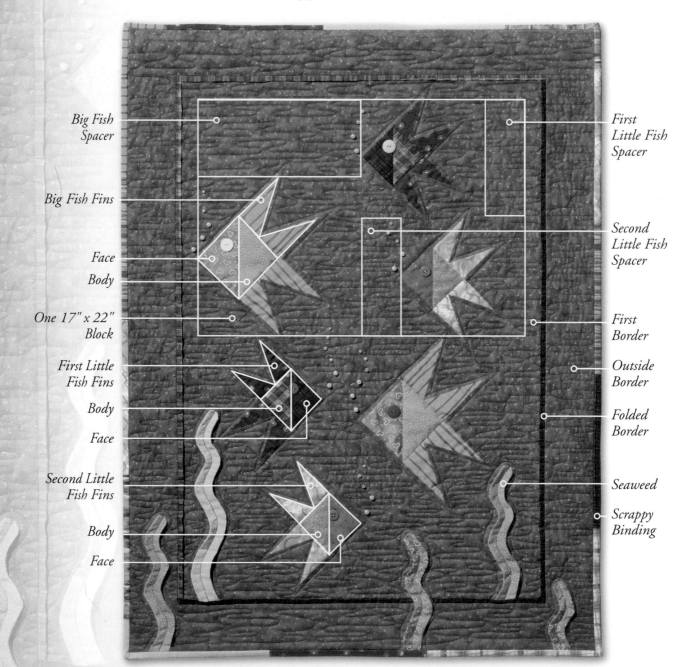

Big Fish Spacer

Big Fish Fins

Face

Body

One 17" x 22" Block

First Little Fish Fins

Body

Face

Second Little Fish Fins

Body

Face

First Little Fish Spacer

Second Little Fish Spacer

First Border

Outside Border

Folded Border

Seaweed

Scrappy Binding

Pieced by Patricia Knoechel
Quilted by Amie Potter
Wallhanging 34" x 45"

Fabric Selection

Select three different bright color families, such as pink, orange, and green. From each color family, select three different textures in different values. Select a total of nine different fabrics for Fish, and a contrasting blue for Water. Fabric left over after Fish are cut can be used for a Scrappy Binding or Folded Border. The Border can be the same as the Water, or a multi-colored print that pulls all colors together.

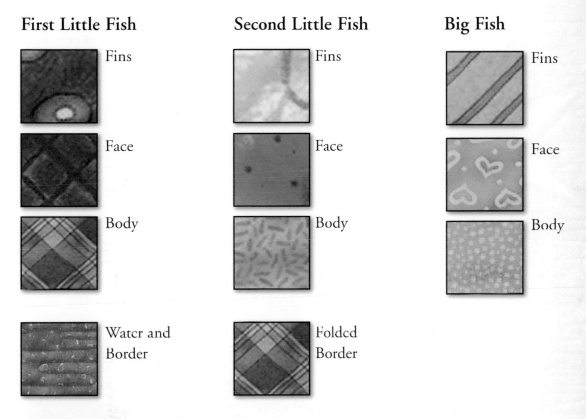

First Little Fish

Fins

Face

Body

Water and Border

Second Little Fish

Fins

Face

Body

Folded Border

Big Fish

Fins

Face

Body

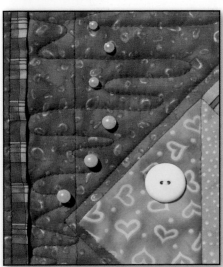

Supplies

Eyes (1) ⅝" Button per Fish
Bubbles 5mm, 6mm, and 8mm Pearls
Triangle in a Square Rulers
(Set includes a Triangle Ruler
and a Squaring Up Ruler.)
12½" Square Up Ruler
4" x 14" Ruler
6½" Triangle Square Up Ruler

Gone Fishing Yardage Chart

Finished Block Size 17" x 22"

			Pillow Case One 17" x 22" Block 20" x 30"	Wallhanging Two 17" x 22" Blocks 34" x 45"
Water			¾ yd	1½ yds
	Little Fish	Corner Triangles	(1) 5½" strip cut into (4) 5½" squares	(2) 5½" strips cut into (8) 5½" squares
		Triangles	(1) 4" x 12"	(1) 4" strip
		Spacers	(1) 3½" strip cut into (2) 3½" x 9"	(2) 3½" strips cut into (4) 3½" x 9"
		Block	(2) 3½" squares	(4) 3½" squares
	Big Fish	Corner Triangles	(1) 7" strip cut into (2) 7" squares	(2) 7" strips cut into (4) 7" squares
		Spacers	(1) 6½" x 12"	(2) 6½" x 12"
		Triangles	(1) 5" x 9"	(1) 5" x 18"
		Block	(1) 4½" square	(2) 4½" squares
	First Border		(3) 2¼" strips	(4) 2" strips
Color Family One			(3) ⅛ yds	(3) ⅛ yds
	Little Fish	Fins	(2) 2½" x 5" from first	(4) 2½" x 5" from first
		Face	(1) 4" square from second	(1) 4" square from second
		Body	(1) 4" square from third	(1) 4" square from third
Color Family Two			(3) ⅛ yds	(3) ⅛ yds
	Little Fish	Fins	(2) 2½" x 5" from first	(4) 2½" x 5" from first
		Face	(1) 4" square from second	(1) 4" square from second
		Body	(1) 4" square from third	(1) 4" square from third
Color Family Three			(3) ¼ yds	(3) ¼ yds
	Big Fish	Fins	(2) 3" x 6" from first	(4) 3" x 6" from first
		Face	(1) 5" square from second	(1) 5" square from second
		Body	(1) 5" square from third	(1) 5" square from third
Seaweed			2 different ⅛ yds	2 different ⅛ yds
Folded Border or Border			⅛ yd (1) 2½" strip	¼ yd (4) 1¼" strips
Outside Border			⅜ yd (1) 12" strip	⅝ yd (4) 4½" strips
One Fabric Binding or Scrappy Binding				⅜ yd (4) 3" strips
Backing			¾ yd	1½ yds
Batting				40" x 52"

Lap 2 x 3 **Six** 17" x 22" Blocks 60" x 66"	Twin 2 x 4 **Eight** 17" x 22" Blocks 63" x 87"	Full/Queen 3 x 5 **Fifteen** 17" x 22" Blocks 92" x 110"
3 yds	3¾ yds	6¾ yds
(4) 5½" strips cut into (24) 5½" squares	(5) 5½" strips cut into (32) 5½" squares	(9) 5½" strips cut into (60) 5½" squares
(1) 4" strip	(2) 4" strips	(4) 4" strips
(4) 3½" strips cut into (12) 3½" x 9"	(6) 3½" strips cut into (16) 3½" x 9"	(10) 3½" strips cut into (30) 3½" x 9"
(12) 3½" squares	(16) 3½" squares	(30) 3½" squares
(3) 7" strips cut into (12) 7" squares	(3) 7" strips cut into (16) 7" squares	(6) 7" strips cut into (30) 7" squares
(2) 6½" strips cut into (6) 6½" x 12"	(3) 6½" strips cut into (8) 6½" x 12"	(5) 6½" strips cut into (15) 6½" x 12"
(1) 5" strip	(1) 5" strip	(3) 5" strips
(6) 4½" squares	(8) 4½" squares	(15) 4½" squares
(6) 2" strips	(8) 2½" strips	(11) 2½" strips
(3) ¼ yds	(3) ¼ yds	(3) ⅓ yds
(12) 2½" x 5" from first	(16) 2½" x 5" from first	(30) 2½" x 5" from first
(3) 4" squares from second	(4) 4" squares from second	(8) 4" squares from second
(3) 4" squares from third	(4) 4" squares from third	(8) 4" squares from third
(3) ¼ yds	(3) ¼ yds	(3) ⅓ yds
(12) 2½" x 5" from first	(16) 2½" x 5" from first	(30) 2½" x 5" from first
(3) 4" squares from second	(4) 4" squares from second	(8) 4" squares from second
(3) 4" squares from third	(4) 4" squares from third	(8) 4" squares from third
(3) ¼ yds	(3) ⅜ yds	(3) ⅝ yds
(12) 3" x 6" from first	(16) 3" x 6" from first	(30) 3" x 6" from first
(3) 5" squares from second	(4) 5" squares from second	(8) 5" squares from second
(3) 5" squares from third	(4) 5" squares from third	(8) 5" squares from third
2 different ⅛ yds	**2 different ⅛ yds**	**2 different ⅛ yds**
¼ yd (6) 1¼" strips	⅓ yd (6) 1½" strips	1¼ yds (9) 4½" strips
1¼ yds (7) 5½" strip	1¾ yds (8) 7" strips	2¼ yds (10) 7" strips
⅔ yd (7) 3" strips	¾ yd (8) 3" strips	1 yd (11) 3" strips
4 yds	5½ yds	10 yds
68" x 74"	70" x 92"	100" x 118"

 **Cutting Fins**

1. Place Fin rectangles **wrong sides together in pairs.**

Number from each family

Pillow Case	1 pair
Wallhanging	2 pairs
Lap	6 pairs
Twin	8 pairs
Full/Queen	15 pairs

Family One  *Family Two* 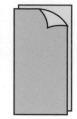 *Family Three*

Little Fish
2½" x 5" rectangles

Big Fish
3" x 6"
rectangles

2. Layer cut pairs on one diagonal.

  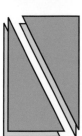

3. Sort triangles right side up.

   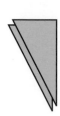 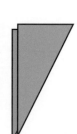 

Cutting Water Triangles

This pattern uses Triangle in a Square Rulers from Quilt in a Day. If you do not own these rulers, make your own templates from Pattern Sheet in back of book.

1. Lay out Water strip right side up. **Accurately line up top of Triangle Ruler with top of strip.** The bottom edge is not as important.

Little Fish 4" Water strip

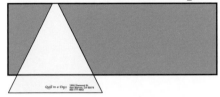

Line up red line on Triangle Ruler with bottom edge of 4" strip.

Big Fish 5" Water strip

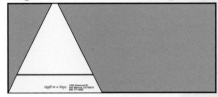

Line up top and bottom edges of ruler with 5" strip.

2. Cut triangles for your size quilt.
   Alternate direction of ruler as you cut.

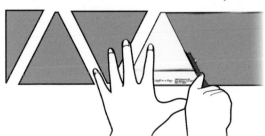

You should get (16) Little Fish triangles per strip, and (12) Big Fish triangles per strip.

	Little Fish	**Big Fish**
Pillow Case	4 triangles	2 triangles
Wallhanging	8 triangles	4 triangles
Lap	24 triangles	12 triangles
Twin	32 triangles	16 triangles
Full/Queen	60 triangles	30 triangles

3. Stack Water triangles right side up with Fin triangles.

 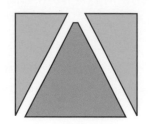 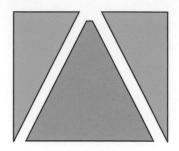

4. Set right Fin triangle stack aside.

 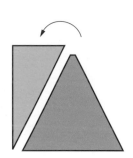 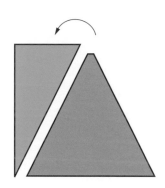

5. Flip Water triangle right sides together to left Fin triangle. Fin triangle extends beyond Water triangle to create a tip at flat top of Water triangle.

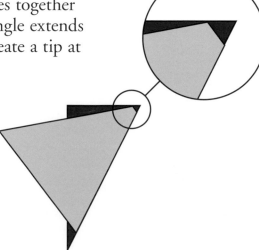

6. Assembly-line sew.

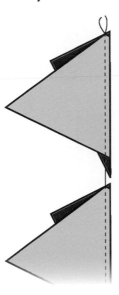

7. Set seams with Fin triangle on top. Open, and press seam toward Fin.

8. Place remaining Fin triangles to right of Water triangles. Flip right sides together.

9. Line top tip of both Fin triangles together. Assembly-line sew.

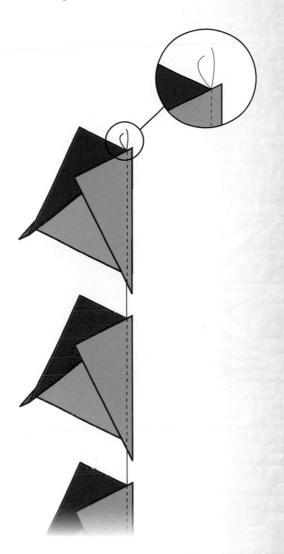

10. Set seams with Fin triangle on top. Open, and press seam toward Fin.

Squaring Little Fish Fins to 3½" Square

1. Using the Triangle in a Square Ruler, line up red triangle lines with seams.

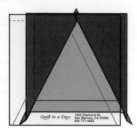

2. Trim patches on two sides.

3. Turn patch. **Do not turn ruler.** Line up red straight lines with freshly cut edges. Trim to 3½" square.

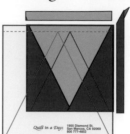

4. Seams are ¼" from top edge, and ⅛" from bottom corners.

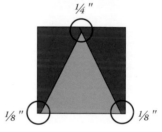

Squaring Big Fish Fins to 4½" Square

1. Place patch on little cutting mat. Place Triangle in a Square Ruler on top of patch. Line up green triangle lines with seams.

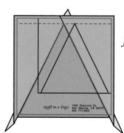

Trim on all four sides.

2. Trim patch on all four sides to 4½" square. Rotate cutting mat as you trim.

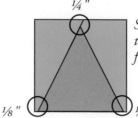

Seams are ¼" from top edge, and ⅛" from bottom corners.

Making Faces and Bodies for Little Fish and Big Fish

1. Place Face fabric and Body fabric squares right sides together.

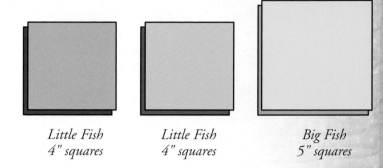

Pillow Case	1 pair from each family
Wallhanging	1 pair from each family
Lap	3 pairs from each family
Twin	4 pairs from each family
Full/Queen	8 pairs from each family

Little Fish 4" squares   *Little Fish 4" squares*   *Big Fish 5" squares*

Each pair of squares makes two Face/Bodies.

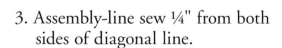

2. On the wrong side of the lightest fabric, draw a diagonal line. Pin.

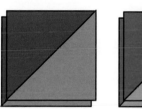

3. Assembly-line sew ¼" from both sides of diagonal line.

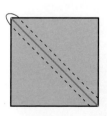

4. Cut apart on drawn line.

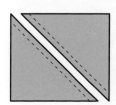

5. Square patches with 6½" Triangle Square Up Ruler.

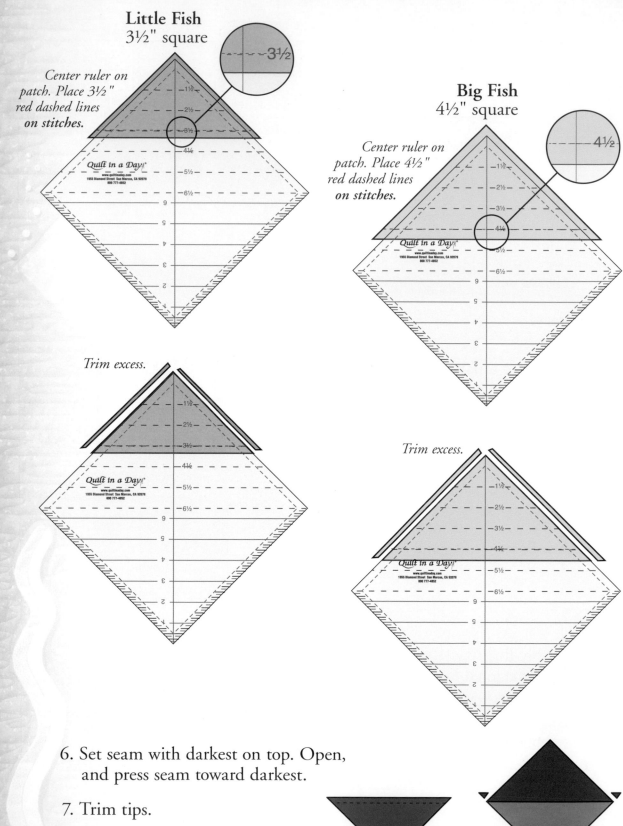

Little Fish
3½" square

Center ruler on patch. Place 3½" red dashed lines on stitches.

Big Fish
4½" square

Center ruler on patch. Place 4½" red dashed lines on stitches.

Trim excess.

Trim excess.

6. Set seam with darkest on top. Open, and press seam toward darkest.

7. Trim tips.

Sewing Block Together

1. Lay out four pieces for one Fish block. Stack Little Fish blocks and Big Fish blocks for assembly-line sewing.

2. Flip blocks on right to blocks on left, right sides together.

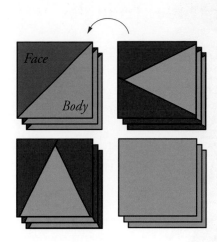

3. Assembly-line sew vertical row. Be careful to sew across X where seams cross.

4. Clip apart every two patches.

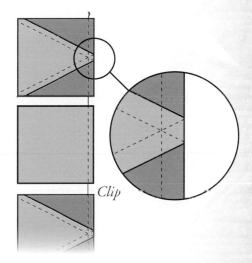

5. Open, and turn. Flip right sides together.

6. Lock center seam, pushing top seam up, and underneath seam down. Assembly-line sew.

7. From wrong side, press seams to one side.

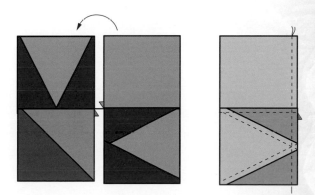

Sewing Side Triangles

1. Cut Water squares in half on one diagonal. Place one triangle on each side of each Fish block. Stack for assembly-line sewing.

2. Flip block right sides together to triangle. Center triangle, and pin.

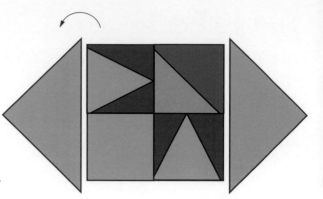

Little Fish	(2) 5½" Water squares per fish
Big Fish	(2) 7" Water squares per fish

3. Sew with triangle on bottom so bias does not stretch.

4. Repeat sewing triangle to opposite side.

5. Set seams with triangles on top. Open, and press seams toward triangles.

6. Trim tips with 4" x 14" ruler.

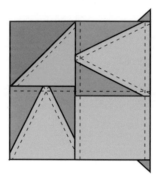

7. Sew triangles to two remaining sides.

8. Set seams with triangles on top. Open, and press seams toward triangles.

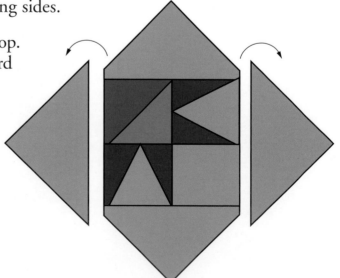

Squaring Blocks

1. Square all blocks to one consistent size. Your blocks may be slightly smaller or larger than suggested sizes.

Little Fish	9"
Big Fish	11¾"

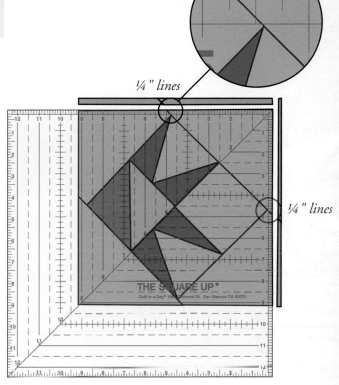

¼ " lines

¼ " lines

2. Line up 12½" Square Up Ruler's diagonal line with center seam. Carefully place ruler's ¼" lines on crossing seams on right and top sides.

3. Trim right and top sides.

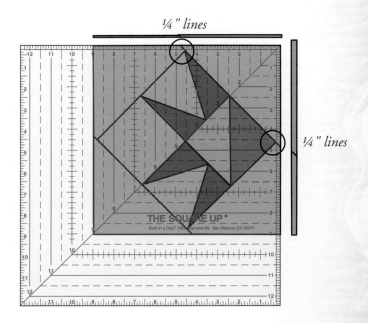

¼ " lines

¼ " lines

4. Turn block. **Do not turn ruler.** Carefully place ruler's ¼" lines on crossing seams on right and top sides. Line up cut edges to edges to squaring size. Trim right and top sides.

Laying Out 17" x 22" Quilt Blocks

Plan arrangements for your blocks. Make one arrangement for each block in your quilt. Fish can swim in opposite direction as well.

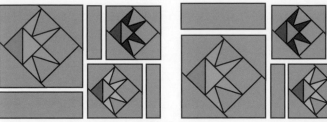

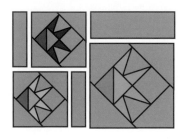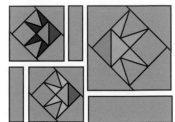

Number of Fish:	Little	Big
Pillow Case	2	1
Wallhanging	4	2
Lap	12	6
Twin	16	8
Full/Queen	30	15

The easiest way is to sew half of the spacers under the Big Fish and half on top of the Big Fish. Sew half of the spacers in front of the Little Fish, and half behind the Little Fish.

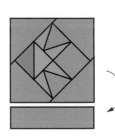

Seaweed: Use this layout for bottom block to allow room for Seaweed.

Sewing Fish Units

1. Place one Big Fish with one 6½" x 12" Spacer above or below Big Fish block.

2. Sew right sides together, sewing through X where seams cross.

3. Press seams toward Spacer. Trim excess Spacer.

4. Select two Little Fish from different Color Families

5. Sew Fish and Spacers right sides together, with Fish on top. Sew through X where seams cross.

6. Press seams toward Spacer. Trim spacers on Little Fish to match width of Big Fish.

7. Sew two Little Fish units together, one on top of the other. Press seam toward top.

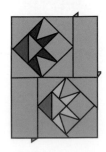

Sewing Top Together

1. Pin and sew two units right sides together.

2. Trim edge of 6½" x 12" Big Fish Spacer so both units are same height.

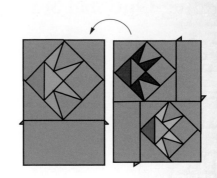

3. Lay out blocks for your size quilt. Press center seams in opposite directions so they lock together.

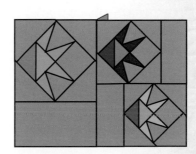

Pillow Case	1 Block
Wallhanging	1 x 2
Lap	2 x 3
Twin	2 x 4
Full/Queen	3 x 5

4. Sew top together.

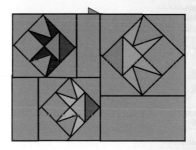

Adding Borders

1. Sew First Border from Water fabric

2. Add Optional Seaweed before and after Folded Border and Border. See Seaweed instructions on page 96.

3. Follow **Folded Border** instructions on page 51.

4. Sew Outside Border. Instructions for **Adding Borders** are on page 230.

Adding Optional Seaweed

Supplies

Template Plastic
Permanent Marking Pen
Fat Drinking Straw
Ball Point Bodkin
Wooden Iron

1. Find Seaweed patterns on Pattern Sheet. Trace Seaweed patterns on template plastic, and cut out.

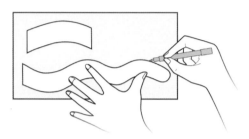

2. Place two different green 4½" Seaweed strips right sides together.

3. **Four Seaweed:** Trace four Seaweed on wrong side of lightest fabric. Leave ½" between each piece. Pin.

4. **One Tall Seaweed:** Tape extender to pattern and trace one tall Seaweed.

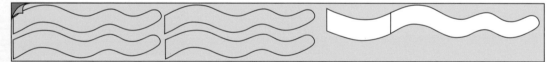

5. Sew on lines with 1.5 or 20 stitches to the inch. Leave open at bottom.

6. Trim ⅛" away from stitches. Clip inside curves.

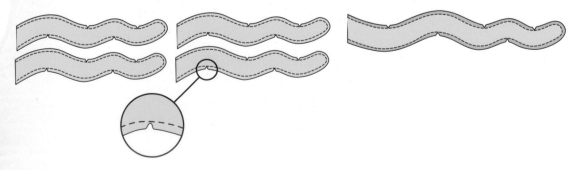

7. Insert straw in opening. Turn right side out by pushing fabric part way into straw with ball point bodkin. Remove straw.

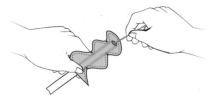

8. Run bodkin around inside to smooth edges.

9. Press edges with iron or wooden iron.

10. Plan placement of Seaweed at bottom of block before Folded Border, and after Border.

11. Trim length of Seaweed as desired, or flip Seaweed over to show second fabric. Pin in place.

12. Double stitch down center of Seaweed through all thicknesses with contrasting thread.

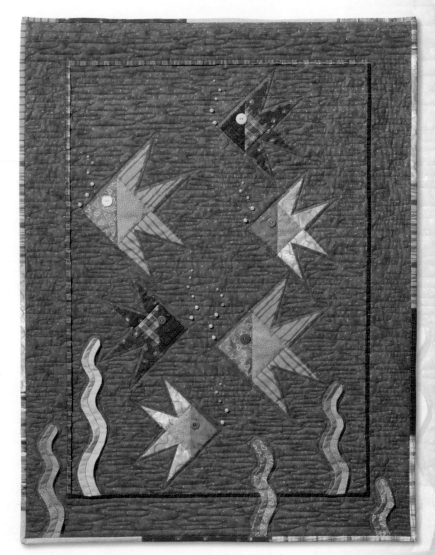

Finishing

1. Turn to **Layering Your Quilt** on page 231.

2. Quilt "Water" with "Wave" stitches.

3. Sew optional pearls for bubbles. For each Fish, sew two 8 mm, two 6 mm, and one 5 mm.

4. Sew optional button eye on each Fish.

Making Pillow Case

1. Make one 17" x 22" Fish Block.

2. Sew 2¼" Water Borders on top and bottom. Press seams toward Borders.

3. Sew 2¼" Border on left only, and press seam toward Border.

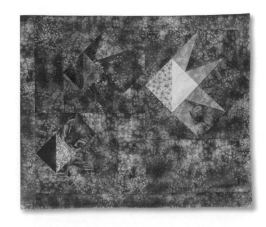

Lining Pillow Case

1. Cut Backing fabric in half on fold.

2. Stack two Backing pieces **right side up**.

3. Place Pillow front **right sides together** to layered Backings. Pin.

4. Layer cut Backings to same size as Pillow front, approximately 21" x 25".

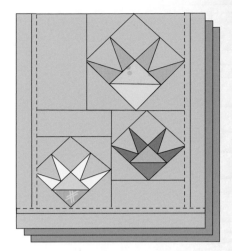

5. Pin around sides and bottom.

6. Backstitch, sew around three sides, and backstitch.

7. Insert hand inside Pillow front, grasp Pillow front, and turn right side out.

8. Pull out corners with stiletto.

9. Lay Pillow Case flat. Measure Pillow Case inside seams and multiply by two. Add ½" for Border seam. Record measurement.

_____"

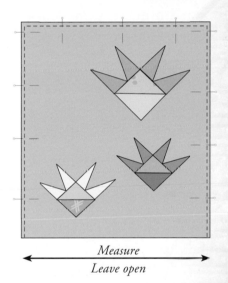

Measure
Leave open

10. Pull Backings apart at open end. Pin one Backing to Pillow front for lining. Baste two together with seam less than ¼". (This Backing lines the patchwork so seams do not fray with washing and wear.)

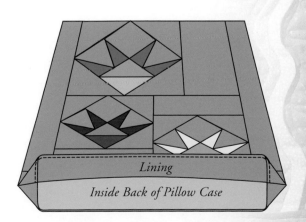

Lining
Inside Back of Pillow Case

Making Pillow Case Borders

1. Press 2½" Folded Border in half length-wise with wrong sides together.

2. Match raw edges of Folded Border and 12" Outside Border. Sew with seam slightly less than ¼".

3. Cut Border at same length as Pillow Case. Refer to #9 on page 99.

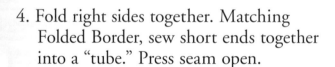

4. Fold right sides together. Matching Folded Border, sew short ends together into a "tube." Press seam open.

5. Refold "tube" wrong sides together. Match raw edges. Baste with seam slightly less than ¼".

6. Slip "tube" over end of Pillow Case right sides together. Match raw edges. Folded Border is on inside of "tube". Place "tube" seam on center back. Pin "tube" and Pillow Case together at four quarter points.

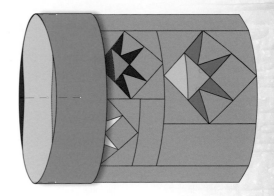

7. Sew "tube" with ¼" seam.

8. Zigzag stitch for a clean finished edge.

9. Fold "tube" out.

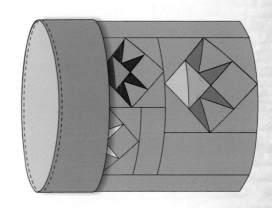

Orion and Eleanor feeding fish and snorkeling in Hawaii.

Twin Sisters Quilts

Twin Sisters is a striking pattern first made in 1845 in Pennsylvania. There is a tragic story concerning this pattern, which was reported by Nancy Cabot, a quilt columnist in the 1930's. A pair of quilts was made for the hope chests of twins. Three weeks before their marriages were to have taken place, one of the twins fell ill and died. The second quilt was passed on to the surviving sister. Eventually, both were passed on to a great granddaughter.

Originally the blocks were made with templates. There is a happy ending to this quilt story, however, as these blocks are now made easily with 2½" half strips. Every pair of 2½" medium and dark half strips makes two blocks — thus twins. The block predominately dark is the **Positive Block**, and the block predominately medium is the **Negative Block**. These small 5" blocks are set together with Lattice and Cornerstones, and are framed with a Rainbow Border.

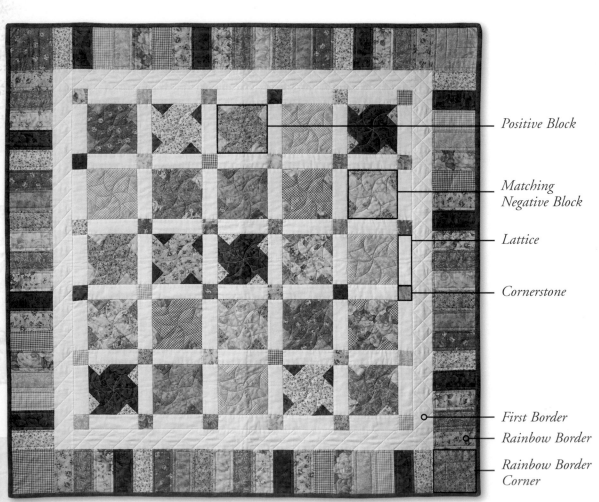

Positive Block

Matching Negative Block

Lattice

Cornerstone

First Border

Rainbow Border

Rainbow Border Corner

Pieced by Teresa Varnes
Quilted by Judy Jackson
47" x 47"

Fabric Selection

Select equal numbers of medium and dark fabrics from your stash or use fat quarters. Pair a medium fabric and a dark fabric together. In addition to having contrast between the two, one fabric should be solid looking with tone on tone texture and the second one should be a small to large scale print.

Purchasing a stack of fat quarters coordinated by your quilt shop or fabric designer/manufacturer from one line is the easiest way of putting fabrics together.

Stash or Fat Quarters

Select values from light medium to dark medium for half of the blocks, and values from dark medium to dark for the second half. Mix scales of prints as well. The more variety there is in color, the easier it is to put blocks together. "Blending" is a good descriptive word, so very different fabrics don't stand out.

If fat quarters are not available, purchase quarter yards, cut on the fold into two 9" x 21" pieces, and proceed as instructed.

Spring Fat Quarters from "Through the Seasons"

For Cornerstones and Rainbow Border, use the same medium and dark fabrics selected for the Blocks.

Lattice

Select a fabric that contrasts with all mediums and darks. Tone on tone white is bright and cheery with pastels. Tone on tone tan is perfect for a country look, and black tone on tone goes well with jewel blocks. Lattice is necessary because blocks do not line up when sewn directly together.

Supplies

Seam Ripper
6½" Triangle Square Up Ruler
6" x 12" Ruler
6" x 24" Ruler

Twin Sisters Yardage Chart

Finished Block Size 5"	Wallhanging 48" x 48" 5 x 5 25 Blocks	Lap 48" x 65" 5 x 8 40 Blocks
Mediums	Stash cut into	Stash cut into
Blocks	(13) 2½" half strips	(20) 2½" half strips
Rainbow Border	(10) 2½" half strips	(13) 2½" half strips
Cornerstones	(18) 2" squares	(27) 2" squares
	or Seven Fat Quarters	**or Seven Fat Quarters**
	Cut from each	Cut from each
Blocks and Rainbow Border	(4) 2½" half strips	(5) 2½" half strips
	Cut from leftovers	Cut from leftovers
Cornerstones	(18) 2" squares	(27) 2" squares
Darks	Stash cut into	Stash cut into
Blocks	(13) 2½" half strips	(20) 2½" half strips
Rainbow Border	(10) 2½" half strips	(13) 2½" half strips
Cornerstones	(18) 2" squares	(27) 2" squares
	or Seven Fat Quarters	**or Seven Fat Quarters**
	Cut from each	Cut from each
Blocks and Rainbow Border	(4) 2½" half strips	(5) 2½" half strips
	Cut from leftovers	Cut from leftovers
Cornerstones	(18) 2" squares	(27) 2" squares
Background	1 yd	1¼ yds
Lattice	(9) 2" strips cut later into (60) 2" x size of block	(14) 2" strips cut later into (93) 2" x size of block
First Border	(4) 2½" strips	(5) 2½" strips
Rainbow Border Corners	¼ yd	¼ yd
	(4) 5" squares or	(4) 5" squares or
	(4) 5" scrappy squares	(4) 5" scrappy squares
Binding	½ yd	⅝ yd
	(5) 3" strips	(6) 3" strips
Backing	3 yds	4 yds
Batting	52" x 52"	52" x 70"

Cutting Instructions on page 106.

Twin	Full/Queen	King
76" x 102"	89" x 102"	102" x 102"
9 x 13	11 x 13	13 x 13
117 Blocks	143 Blocks	169 Blocks

Stash cut into	Stash cut into	Stash cut into
(59) 2½" half strips	(72) 2½" half strips	(85) 2½" half strips
(30) 2½" half strips	(30) 2½" half strips	(30) 2½" half strips
(70) 2" squares	(84) 2" squares	(98) 2" squares
or Fifteen Fat Quarters	**or Seventeen Fat Quarters**	**or Twenty Fat Quarters**
Cut from each	Cut from each	Cut from each
(6) 2½" half strips	(6) 2½" half strips	(6) 2½" half strips
Cut from leftovers	Cut from leftovers	Cut from leftovers
(70) 2" squares	(84) 2" squares	(98) 2" squares
Stash cut into	**Stash cut into**	**Stash cut into**
(59) 2½" half strips	(72) 2½" half strips	(85) 2½" half strips
(30) 2½" half strips	(30) 2½" half strips	(30) 2½" half strips
(70) 2" squares	(84) 2" squares	(98) 2" squares
or Fifteen Fat Quarters	**or Seventeen Fat Quarters**	**or Twenty Fat Quarters**
Cut from each	Cut from each	Cut from each
(6) 2½" half strips	(6) 2½" half strips	(6) 2½" half strips
Cut from leftovers	Cut from leftovers	Cut from leftovers
(70) 2" squares	(84) 2" squares	(98) 2" squares
3 yds	3½ yds	4 yds
(37) 2" strips cut later into	(45) 2" strips cut later into	(52) 2" strips cut later into
(256) 2" x size of block	(310) 2" x size of block	(364) 2" x size of block
(8) 2½" strips	(8) 2½" strips	(9) 2½" strips
¼ yd	¼ yd	¼ yd
(4) 6½" Corner squares or	(4) 6½" Corner squares or	(4) 6½" Corner squares or
(4) 6½" scrappy squares	(4) 6½" scrappy squares	(4) 6½" scrappy squares
1 yd	1 yd	1 yd
(10) 3" strips	(10) 3" strips	(11) 3" strips
6½ yds	9 yds	9½ yds
84" x 110"	97" x 110"	110" x 110"

Cutting 2½" Strips from Stash

1. Half strips for Blocks need to be at least 19" long.

2. Layer cut extra fabric into 2" strips for Cornerstones.

3. Cut 2" strips into 2" squares until you have total number of Cornerstones needed.

Cutting 2½" Strips from Fat Quarters

1. Coordinate medium and dark fat quarters into pairs. Place right sides together.

2. Place coordinated pairs on cutting mat, right sides together, with dark on top. Press. Layer three to four sets.

3. Straighten left edge. Layer cut 2½" strip sets according to your yardage chart. Strips are now right sides together in pairs, and ready for sewing.

4. Layer cut extra fabric into 2" strips for Cornerstones.

5. Cut 2" strips into 2" squares until you have total number of Cornerstones needed. Cut half from medium and half from dark.

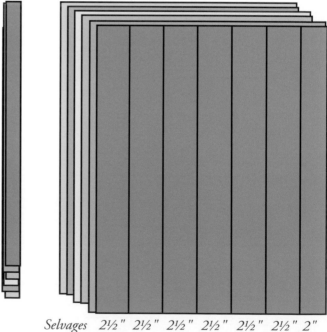

Number of 2" Squares	
Wallhanging	36
Lap	54
Twin	140
Full/Queen	168
King	196

Selvages   2½" 2½" 2½" 2½" 2½" 2½" 2"

Sewing Strips Together

1. If half strips are not already in pairs, select one medium and one dark half strip that coordinate. Place cut edges at top.

2. Flip dark strip onto medium strip, right sides together, and sew with a ¼" seam.

3. Repeat sewing a variety of medium/dark pairs until you have the number needed.

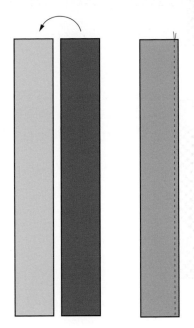

Number of Medium/ Dark Pairs	
Wallhanging	13
Lap	20
Twin	59
Full/Queen	72
King	85

Sew pairs for blocks. Set Rainbow Border strips aside.

4. Set aside remaining Rainbow Border strips.

Number of Medium/Dark	Pairs for Border
Wallhanging	10
Lap	13
Twin	30
Full/Queen	30
King	30

5. Set seam with dark on top, open, and press seam toward dark.

6. Measure width of strips. Strips should measure 4½". If your measurement is different, use your measurement for cutting squares.

Your measurement _____ "

← 4½" →

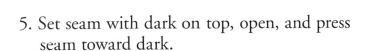

Cutting Strips into Squares

You must be consistent in all steps.

1. Line up three to four strip sets on cutting mat. Always place dark across top, and selvage edge on right. **Do not stack strips.**

2. Square off left ends with 6" x 24" Ruler.

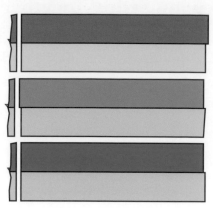

Place Dark across top.

3. Cut each strip set into four 4½" squares, or to your measurement. Separate blocks about ½" after each cut. Leave squares lying on cutting mat.

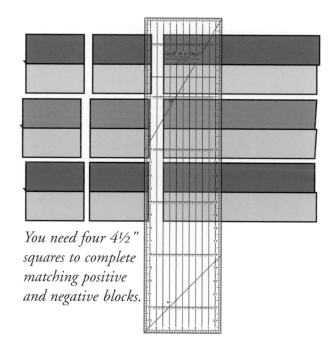

You need four 4½" squares to complete matching positive and negative blocks.

4. With 6" x 12" Ruler, **consistently** cut squares on one diagonal. **Do not stack squares for layer cutting.**

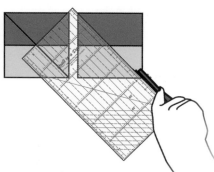

If you are right handed, cut as illustrated.

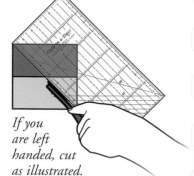

If you are left handed, cut as illustrated.

Stacking Blocks

1. Separate triangles in row.

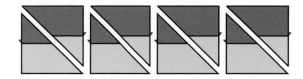

2. Make two stacks with identical pieces.

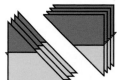

One stack is mostly dark for Positive Blocks.

One stack is mostly medium for Negative Blocks.

3. Take left stack of four identical pieces. Lay out negative block with medium dominate. The 90° angle always goes in center.

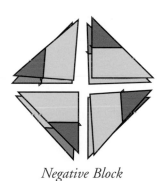

Negative Block

4. Take right stack of four identical pieces. Lay out positive block with dark dominate. The 90° angle always goes in center.

5. Continue to cut squares on diagonal, sort, and stack on positive or negative block.

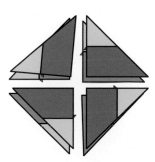

Positive Block

For assembly-line sewing, stack more blocks on top of the first block.

Sewing Blocks Together

1. Work on one stack of blocks at a time.

2. Flip pieces on right to pieces on left.

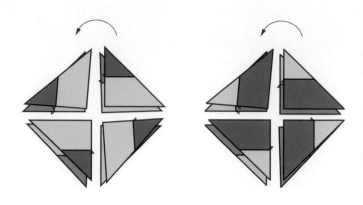

3. Matching outside edges, assembly-line sew. Use stiletto to hold outside edges together and seams flat.

4. Repeat with all pieces in stack. **Clip apart every two pieces, and open.**

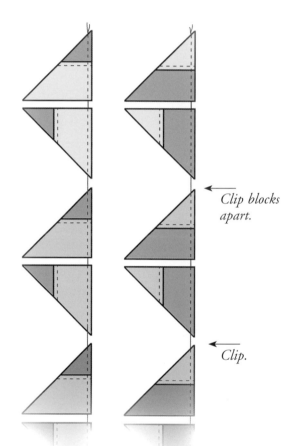

Clip blocks apart.

Clip.

5. Turn block.

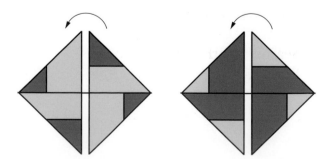

110

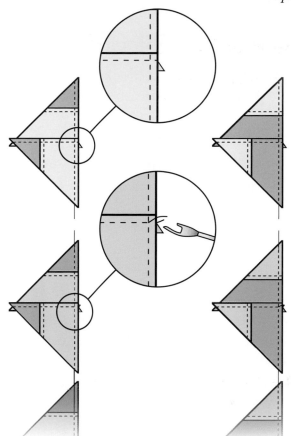

6. Sew remaining seam, pushing top seam up, and underneath seam down. Repeat with all blocks.

7. Cut blocks apart, and stack.

8. Clip connecting thread with seam ripper.

Press seam to right.

Press seam up. *Press seam down.*

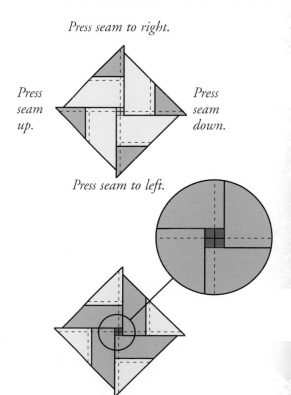

Press seam to left.

9. Open and place wrong side up on pressing mat. Press top vertical seam to right. Press bottom vertical seam to left. Center seam pops open. Finger press seams.

10. Flatten center, creating a small four-patch. Press seams flat from wrong side. Seams "swirl" around center four-patch. The outside edges are on the bias. Press carefully so block does not stretch.

Check Size of Block

1. Measure several blocks. Approximate size should be 5½".

    Record Size _____

2. If blocks are consistent size, it is not necessary to square up blocks.

3. Trim tips even with block.

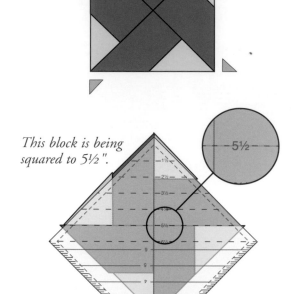

Squaring Up Block

1. If blocks vary in size, they should be squared to one consistent size.

2. Square up to smallest consistent size with 6½" Triangle Square Up Ruler.

    Record Size _____

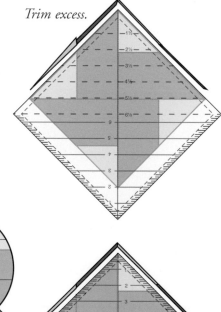

This block is being squared to 5½".

3. Place horizontal line of smallest consistent measurement **on seam**. Place vertical line on vertical seam.

4. Trim two sides.

5. Turn patch. **Do not turn ruler.** Place horizontal line of smallest consistent measurement **on seam**. Place vertical line on vertical seam. Trim remaining two sides.

Trim excess.

6. If block size is different than 5½" as 5¼", turn ruler around with solid green lines at top, and trim.

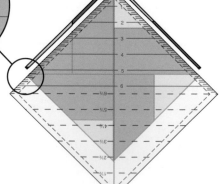

Cutting Lattice

1. Place 2" Lattice strips on cutting mat. Trim selvage edge.

2. Layer cut into strips same size as your block.

Number of Lattice	
Wallhanging	60
Lap	93
Twin	256
Full/Queen	310
King	364

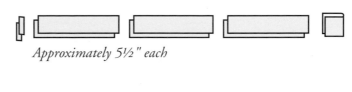

Approximately 5½" each

Laying Out Blocks

1. Divide blocks into two piles with Positive Blocks in one pile, and Negative Blocks in second pile.

Number of Blocks in each pile	
Wallhanging	13
Lap	20
Twin	59
Full/Queen	72
King	85

 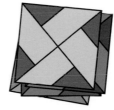

Positive Block   *Negative Block*

2. Begin with Positive Block. Lay out blocks in rows in alternating positive/negative order.

Rows Across and Down	
Wallhanging	5 x 5
Lap	5 x 8
Twin	9 x 13
Full/Queen	11 x 13
King	13 x 13

3. Leave 2" space between blocks for Lattice and Cornerstones.

4. Begin each row with the first block the opposite of block in row above it.

5. Place 2" Lattice and 2" Cornerstones between blocks.

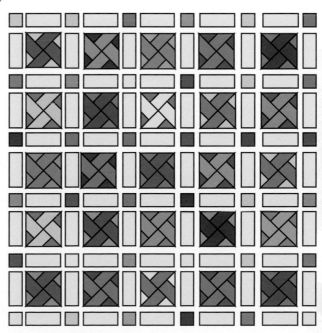

Example of Wallhanging 5 x 5

113

Sewing Top Together

1. Flip second vertical row right sides together to first vertical row.

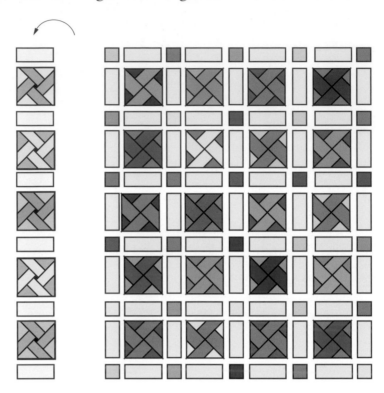

2. Stack from bottom up with top Lattice on top of stack.

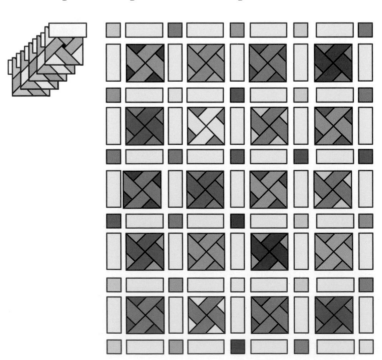

3. Assembly-line sew. Stretch or ease each block to fit the Lattice as you sew. **Do not clip connecting threads.**

4. Open vertical rows one and two.

5. Stack third vertical row. Flip pieces in third vertical row right sides together to pieces in second vertical row. Assembly-line sew. Do not clip connecting threads.

6. Repeat with remaining vertical rows.

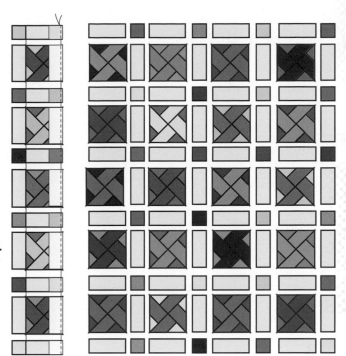

Sewing Horizontal Rows

1. Flip top horizontal row right sides together to second horizontal row. Stretch or ease blocks and Lattice to fit, and sew.

2. At Cornerstones where pieces are joined by threads, match seams carefully. Push seams toward Lattice for locking seams.

3. Continue sewing all horizontal rows.

4. Press seams toward Lattice from wrong side. Press from right side.

5. Add First Border from Background. Turn to page 230.

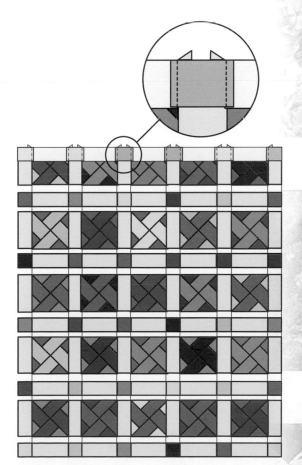

Push seams toward Lattice for locking seams.

Rainbow Border

1. Count out 2½" medium half strips and 2½" dark half strips.

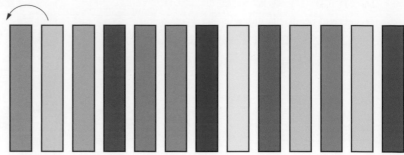

Example of a Lap with (13) 2½" half strips. Make two sets.

2. Sew 2½" half strips together lengthwise with ¼" seam, alternating medium and dark.

Number of Sets

Wallhanging	1 set of 20
Lap	2 sets of 13 each
Twin	4 sets of 15 each
Full/Queen	4 sets of 15 each
King	4 sets of 15 each

3. Press seams in one direction.

4. Fold in half lengthwise. Square left edge. Cut each set into sections.

Section Measurements

Wallhanging	5"
Lap	5"
Twin	6½"
Full/Queen	6½"
King	6½"

Wallhanging and Lap

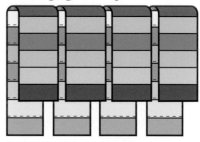

Cut four 5" sections from each.

Twin, Full/Queen, King

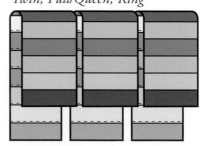

Cut three 6½" sections from each.

5. Piece together end to end into one long piece.

Finishing

1. Measure strips against four sides. Remove strips the same length as sides from long strip. If necessary, sew a few deeper seams until Rainbow Borders fit.

2. Place seams in same direction as you are sewing. Pin and sew to sides. Press seams toward First Border.

3. Sew 5" or 6½" Corners to both ends of top and bottom. Press seams toward Corners.

4. Pin and sew Rainbow Border to top and bottom. Press seams toward First Border.

5. Turn to **Layering Your Quilt** on page 231.

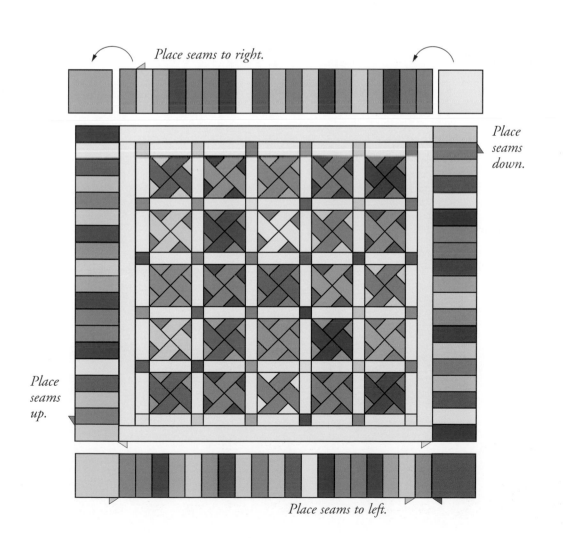

Place seams to right.

Place seams down.

Place seams up.

Place seams to left.

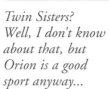

*Twin Sisters?
Well, I don't know
about that, but
Orion is a good
sport anyway...*

Oh Baby!

Eleanor chose traditional pastels
for her sweet baby quilt. The soft
shades are echoed in her cornerstones and piano key border. The
overall effect is enhanced by her use
of white lattice and framing border.

*Pieced by Eleanor Burns
Quilted by Amie Potter
48" x 48"*

Pieced by Sue Bouchard
Quilted by Amie Potter
48" x 65"

Twin Sisters

Sue chose rich pastels for her scrappy quilt. She used dark and medium to light strips in each block for contrast. Her quilt has a vintage look with her use of white lattice and pieced border.

Oops, My Passion is Showing

Lois loves cheery bright colors and this pattern is perfect for her to indulge that passion. She used black for her lattice and border to give her quilt a striking appeal.

Pieced and quilted
by Lois Bretzloff
45" x 64"

Baskets and Bows Quilt

Baskets and Bows is colorful with repeated **Flower Baskets** set on point in vertical rows with Side and Corner Triangles. Vertical Basket rows are framed with 3½" Lattice stripes embellished with charming country Bows.

Putting together blocks is like filling a basket with hand picked flowers. Begin with large flowers in beautiful pinks, yellows, blues, and purples. Fill in with smaller flowers in accent colors. Last, freshen with leaves right from nature.

Corner Triangle

Large Scale Floral

Side Triangle

Striped Lattice and Border

Basket

Background

Block

Appliqued Flowers and Leaves

Pieced by Patricia Knoechel
Quilted by Amie Potter
31" x 39"

Fabric Selection

1168-33

Large Scale Floral
Select fabric with clusters of flowers 4" to 5" wide to fussy cut into a triangle shape for the top of the Basket. Additional flowers can be appliqued onto the fussy cut triangle to complete the bouquet. When purchasing fabric, count out one "fussy cut" for each Basket in your size quilt.

1172-33

Background
Select fabric that matches the Background of the Large Scale Floral as a tone on tone, or a small scale print with flowers the same colors as flowers in the Large Scale Floral.

1167-55

Basket
Select a small check or basket weave print in a natural color or cheery bright.

1166-55

Side and Corner Triangles
Select a tone on tone in a color pulled from the Large Scale Floral that compliments the other colors, but which contrasts with the Background. For variety, select a different scale print.

1169-33

Striped Lattice and Border
Select a stripe approximately 3½" wide for Lattice. The stripe fabric in this quilt has repeated stripes across the width of the fabric.

Non-Woven Fusible Interfacing
Select non-woven light to medium weight fusible interfacing. One side of the interfacing is smooth in texture, while the other side has fusible dots. Do not confuse this interfacing with paper backed webbed fusing. Fusible interfacing is used to turn under raw edges of applique.

Supplies

9½" Square Up Ruler
6½" Fussy Cut Ruler
OR 6½" Triangle Square Up Ruler

Baskets and Bows Yardage Chart

Finished Block Size 8½"		Tablerunner 4 Baskets 20" x 68"	Wallhanging 6 Baskets 31" x 39"
Large Scale Floral		½ yd	½ yd
		(1) 6½" strip cut into (4) 6½" squares (1) 4½" square OR	(1) 6½" strip cut into (6) 6½" squares OR
		(4) 6½" Fussy Cuts	(6) 6½" Fussy Cuts
		(1) 4½" Fussy Cut	
Background		½ yd	½ yd
	Top	(1) 1½" strip cut into (4) 1½" x 6½"	(1) 1½" strip cut into (6) 1½" x 6½"
	Top	(1) 1½" strip cut into (4) 1½" x 7½"	(2) 1½" strips cut into (6) 1½" x 7½"
	Sides	(2) 2¼" strips cut into (8) 2¼" x 6"	(2) 2¼" strips cut into (12) 2¼" x 6"
	Bottom	(2) 5½" squares Center Block (2) 4½" squares	(1) 4½" strip cut into (3) 4½" squares
Basket		⅓ yd	⅓ yd
	Basket	(1) 6½" strip cut into (2) 6½" squares (2) 4½" squares Center Block	(1) 6½" strip cut into (3) 6½" squares
	Feet	(1) 2½" strip cut into (4) 2½" squares	(1) 2½" strip cut into (6) 2½" squares
Side and Corner Triangles		½ yd	⅔ yd
	Sides	(2) 13½" squares	(2) 13½" squares
	Corners	(2) 7½" squares	(4) 7½" squares
Striped Lattice		2¼ yds (4) 3½" lengthwise strips	1½ yds (6) 3½" lengthwise strips
First Border		——	——
Second Border (Non-stripe)		——	——
Non-Woven Fusible Interfacing		¼ yd	¼ yd
Binding		½ yd (5) 3" strips	½ yd (4) 3" strips
Backing		2 yds	1¼ yds
Batting		24" x 72"	36" x 45"

Instructions for Fussy Cutting Large Scale Floral on page 124.

Lap 15 Baskets 48" x 64"	Twin 18 Baskets 74" x 105"	Full/Queen 24 Baskets 89" x 105"	King 30 Baskets 105" x 105"
1 yd	1⅛ yds	1¾ yds	2 yds
(3) 6½" strips cut into (15) 6½" squares OR	(3) 6½" strips cut into (18) 6½" squares OR	(4) 6½" strips cut into (24) 6½" squares OR	(5) 6½" strips cut into (30) 6½" squares OR
(15) 6½" Fussy Cuts	(18) 6½" Fussy Cuts	(24) 6½" Fussy Cuts	(30) 6½" Fussy Cuts
¾ yd	1 yd	1¼ yds	1½ yds
(3) 1½" strips cut into (15) 1½" x 6½"	(3) 1½" strips cut into (18) 1½" x 6½"	(4) 1½" strips cut into (24) 1½" x 6½"	(5) 1½" strips cut into (30) 1½" x 6½"
(3) 1½" strips cut into (15) 1½" x 7½"	(4) 1½" strips cut into (18) 1½" x 7½"	(5) 1½" strips cut into (24) 1½" x 7½"	(6) 1½" strips cut into (30) 1½" x 7½"
(5) 2¼" strips cut into (30) 2¼" x 6"	(6) 2¼" strips cut into (36) 2¼" x 6"	(8) 2¼" strips cut into (48) 2¼" x 6"	(10) 2¼" strips cut into (60) 2¼" x 6"
(1) 4½" strip cut into (8) 4½" squares	(2) 4½" strips cut into (9) 4½" squares	(2) 4½" strips cut into (12) 4½" squares	(2) 4½" strips cut into (15) 4½" squares
½ yd	¾ yd	⅝ yd	⅞ yd
(2) 6½" strips cut into (8) 6½" squares	(2) 6½" strips cut into (9) 6½" squares	(2) 6½" strips cut into (12) 6½" squares	(3) 6½" strips cut into (15) 6½" squares
(1) 2½" strip cut into (15) 2½" squares	(2) 2½" strips cut into (18) 2½" squares	(2) 2½" strips cut into (24) 2½" squares	(2) 2½" strips cut into (30) 2½" squares
1½ yds	1¾ yds	2 yds	2½ yds
(2) 13½" strips cut into (6) 13½" squares	(3) 13½" strips cut into (8) 13½" squares	(4) 13½" strips cut into (10) 13½" squares	(5) 13½" strips cut into (13) 13½" squares
(2) 7½" strips cut into (6) 7½" squares	(2) 7½" strips cut into (6) 7½" squares	(2) 7½" strips cut into (8) 7½" squares	(2) 7½" strips cut into (10) 7½" squares
2 yds (6) 3½" lengthwise strips	2¼ yds (6) 3½" lengthwise strips	2¼ yds (7) 3½" lengthwise strips	2¼ yds (8) 3½" lengthwise strips
———	1⅛ yds (7) 5" strips	1¼ yds (8) 5" strips	1¼ yds (8) 5" strips
———	2½ yds (9) 9" strips	2¾ yds (10) 9" strips	3 yds (11) 9" strips
½ yd	½ yd	1 yd	1 yd
¾ yd (6) 3" strips	1 yd (9) 3" strips	1 yd (10) 3" strips	1 yd (11) 3" strips
4 yds	6½ yds	9½ yds	9½ yds
54" x 70"	80" x 110"	96" x 110"	110" x 110"

Cutting Fussy Cut Flower Triangles

1. Make photocopy of Template A, and cut out. Find template on Pattern Sheet.

2. Turn 6½" Triangle Square Up Ruler or 6½" Fussy Cut Ruler to underneath side. Tape template to corner of ruler.

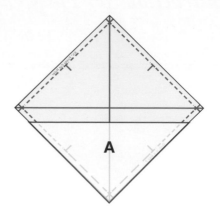

3. Center marked ruler on Flower to fussy cut.

4. Mark fabric on both sides of template.

   If you cut 6½" squares, place Template A on corner of square, draw lines, and cut on line.

Mark fabric on both sides.

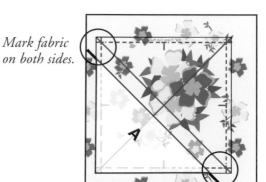

5. Rotary cut around triangle. Cut straight line between two marks with 6" x 12" Ruler.

6. Cut one Flower for each Basket in your quilt. For variety, select several different flower arrangements.

7. Save leftover scraps to fill in Baskets.

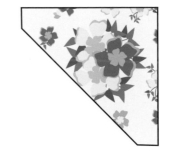

8. If you don't have a 6½" Ruler, trace Template B on template plastic, and cut out. Place on fussy cut, trace around Template B with permanent marking pen and rotary cut with 6" x 12" Ruler.

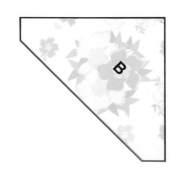

Making Baskets

1. Cut 6½" Basket squares in half on one diagonal. Each square is enough for two Baskets.

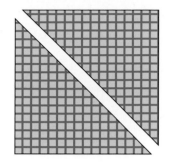

Number of 6" Squares

Tablerunner	2
Wallhanging	3
Lap	8
Twin	9
Full/Queen	12
King	15

2. Place Basket with Flower.

3. Flip right sides together, and **center Basket** on Flower with tips extending equally on both sides. Assembly-line sew.

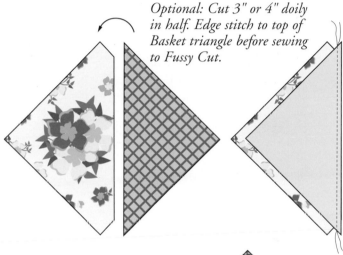

Optional: Cut 3" or 4" doily in half. Edge stitch to top of Basket triangle before sewing to Fussy Cut.

4. Set seam with Basket on top. Open and press seam toward Basket.

5. Place 6½" Ruler on patch. Line up edge of ruler with edge of Flower. Trim Basket to 6½".

6. If you don't have a 6½" Ruler, use 9½" Square Up Ruler.

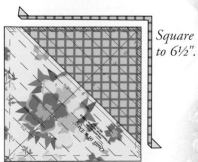

Square to 6½".

Sometimes the Fussy Cut shrinks about ⅛" with pressing and sewing. If this happens, just gently stretch it to meet the strips added next.

7. Stack 1½" x 6½" Background strips to right of Flowers. Flip right sides together.

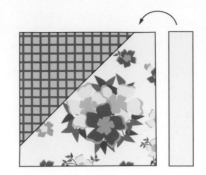

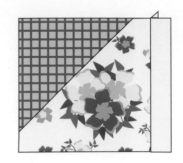

8. Assembly-line sew, matching edges.

9. Set seam with strip on top, open, and press seam toward strip.

10. Stack 1½" x 7½" Background strips to right of Flowers. Flip right sides together and assembly-line sew.

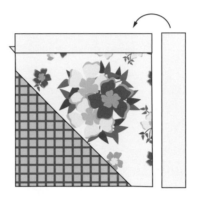

11. Press seam toward strip. If necessary, trim strip to match Basket.

Sewing Basket Feet

1. Cut 2½" Basket Feet in half on one diagonal.

2. Stack Feet next to equal stacks of 2¼" x 6" Background strips. Make a set for each Basket.

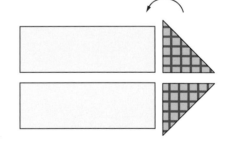

3. Flip right sides together. Match 90° angles, and assembly-line sew.

4. Press seams toward Feet.

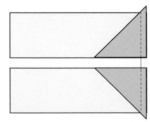

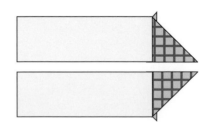

5. Place Feet to right side of Basket. Line up top edges.

6. Flip right sides together, and assembly-line sew. Tip extends approximately ½" at bottom.

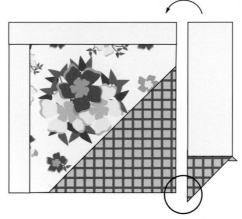

Tip extends approximately ½".

7. Set seam with Side on top, open, and press toward Side. Trim tip at bottom.

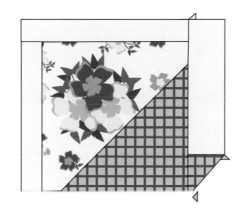

8. Rotate the block. Place Feet with Basket. Line up straight edges, and assembly-line sew. Tip extends approximately ¼".

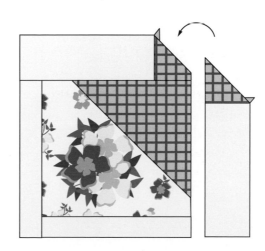

9. Set seam with Side on top, open, and press toward Side.

10. Straighten bottom edge, leaving ¼" seam allowance.

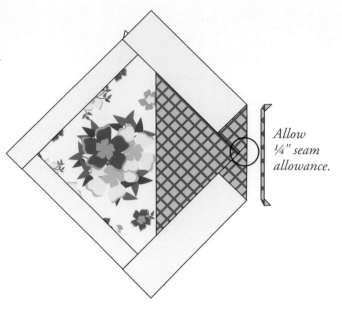

Allow ¼" seam allowance.

11. Cut 4½" Background squares in half on one diagonal.

12. Stack Background triangles with Baskets. Flip right sides together, letting tips hang over equally on both sides.

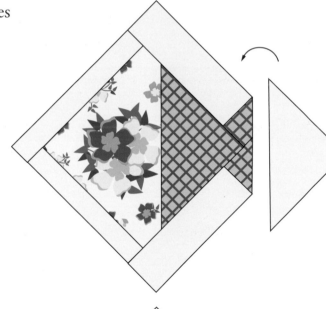

13. Turn over. Stitch across X at bottom of Basket.

14. Set seam with Background on top, open, and press toward Background.

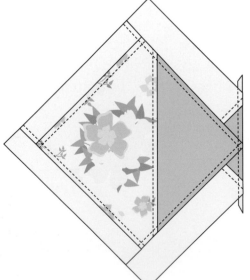

15. Place 9½" Square Up Ruler on Basket. Trim Background triangle. Remember to leave at least ¼" seam. Block should square to approximately 9".

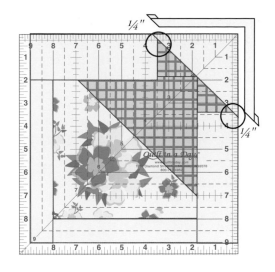

One Block Wallhanging

Make one extra block, sewing lace to Basket before Fussy Cut. For Side Triangles, cut two 7½" squares in half on one diagonal, and sew to block. Cut four 2" x 21" strips for mitered Borders. Follow Mitering instructions on page 224.

Pieced by Patricia Knoechel
Quilted by Amie Potter
18" x 18"

Appliqueing Additional Flowers

To complete a flower or leaf that was cut off in the fussy cut, select an identical piece and make it into a paper backed fusible applique or fusible interfacing applique. Overlap replacement piece on seam of Basket and Side strips.

Paper Backed Fusible Applique

1. Rough cut around selected flower or leaf. Cut paper slightly smaller than fabric so you don't get fusible on your iron or mat. Place wrong side of fabric against fusible side of paper.

2. Fuse together following manufacturer's directions.

3. Cut outline of fabric flower or leaf. Peel off paper backing.

4. Fuse in place.

Fusible Interfacing Applique

1. Rough cut around selected flower or leaf. Turn fabric wrong side up, and trace outline of shape with a fine permanent pen. If necessary, simplify shape for ease of sewing.

2. Place right side of fabric against fusible side of non-woven fusible interfacing, and pin.

3. Sew on drawn line with needle down and 20 stitches per inch. Trim ⅛" away. Clip inside curves.

4. Cut slit in back, turn and stuff with 100% cotton batting. See pages 53 and 54.

5. Steam press in place.

6. Hand or machine sew outside edges before machine quilting or when machine quilting.

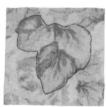

Making Center Block for Tablerunner

1. Cut two 4½" Basket squares and two 5½" Background squares in half on one diagonal.

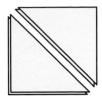

4½" square   *5½" square*

2. Place one Basket triangle on each side of 4½" Fussy Cut square.

3. Sew with triangles on bottom so bias does not stretch.

4. Press seams toward triangles. Trim tips.

5. Sew Basket triangles to two remaining sides. Press seams toward triangles.

6. Square to 6½" with Fussy Cut Ruler.

7. Repeat with Background triangles.

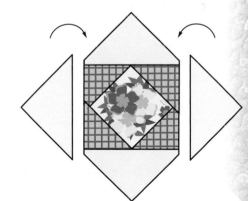

8. Square to same size as Basket block.

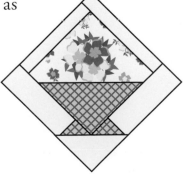

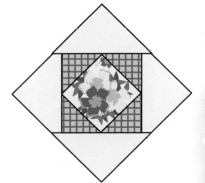

Sewing Vertical Rows Together

1. Cut 13½" squares for Side Triangles on both diagonals.

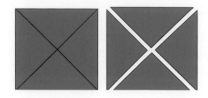

2. Lay out blocks with Side Triangles.

Number of Baskets and Rows

Tablerunner	4 Baskets, 1 Row
Wallhanging	3 Baskets, 2 Rows
Lap	5 Baskets, 3 Rows
Twin	6 Baskets, 3 Rows
Full/Queen	6 Baskets, 4 Rows
King	6 Baskets, 5 Rows

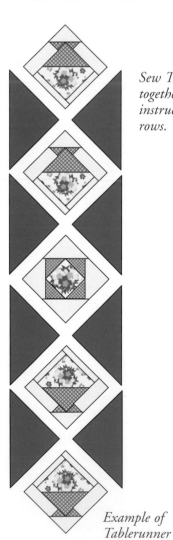

Sew Tablerunner together following instructions for quilt rows.

Example of Tablerunner

Example of Lap Row

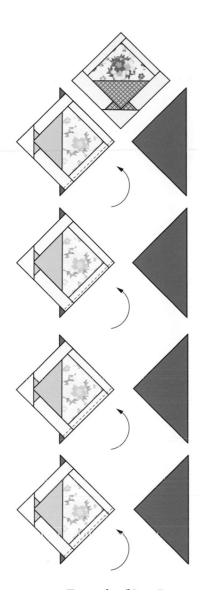

Example of Lap Row

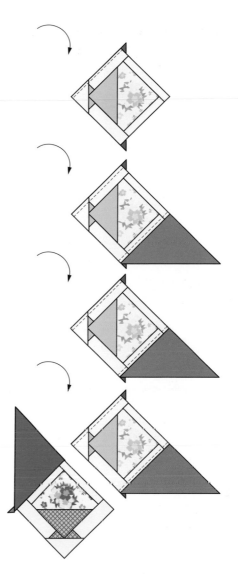

3. Starting with second block from top, flip blocks up to the left. Match square corners and pin with tip extending. Stack paired blocks and assembly-line sew with triangle on bottom to prevent bias from stretching.

4. Clip blocks apart, and press seams toward triangles. Return to layout.

5. Starting at the top, flip blocks down to the right. Leave last block in layout. Match up square corners and pin. Stack paired blocks from bottom up, and assembly-line sew, starting from the square corners.

6. Clip blocks apart, and press seams toward triangles.

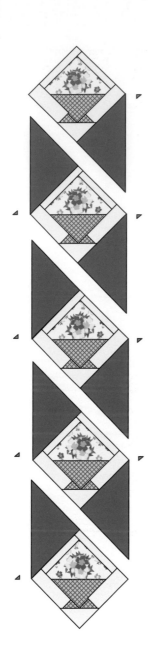

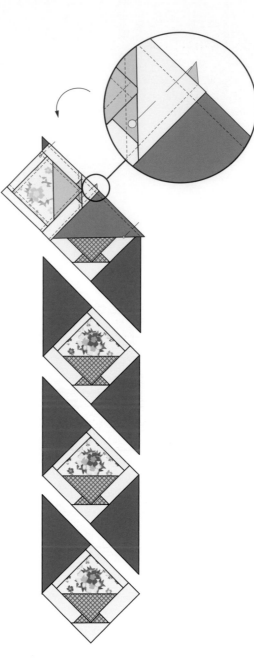

7. Trim tips even with blocks.

8. Return to layout.

9. Flip top row down to second row. Match center seam, pin, and sew. Continue adding remaining rows.

10. Press diagonal seams down toward bottom of quilt. Trim tips even with blocks.

Adding Corner Triangles

1. Cut two 7½" Corner squares in half on one diagonal.

2. Fold triangles in half and press. Open.

3. Fold top and bottom blocks on two opposite corners in half, press, and open. Pin center of triangle to center of block. Let tips hang over on ends. Pin.

4. Sew triangles to two opposite corners with triangles on bottom.

5. Set seams with triangle on top, open, and press seams toward triangles. Trim tips.

6. Repeat with remaining two corners.

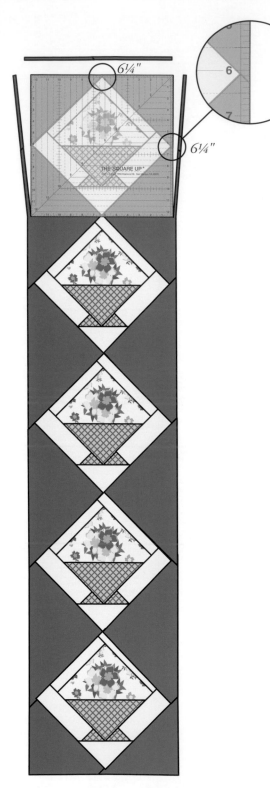

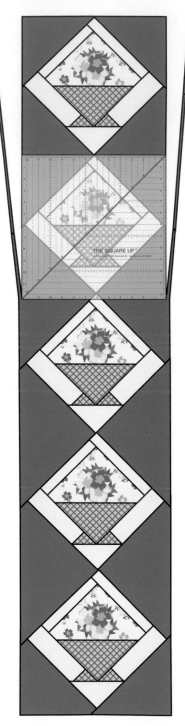

7. Place Quilt in a Day's 12½" Square Up Ruler in upper right corner. Place ruler's ¼" marks on points.

8. Trim corners.

9. Line up rulers' diagonal line with seams, and trim ¼" from points where seams cross.

Cutting Lattice

1. Lay out vertical rows of Baskets.

2. Measure length of rows, and cut 3½" Lattice strips slightly longer. If necessary, piece strips together to get length.

3. Place Lattice on right side of vertical rows, consistently placing pattern.

4. Pin and sew Lattice to vertical rows, lining up pattern straight across.

5. Sew Lattice to left side of first row.

6. Trim Lattice to length of rows. Press seams toward Lattice.

7. Sew Lattice to top and bottom, trim, and press seam toward Lattice.

8. **Twin, Full/Queen, King:** Turn to **Adding Borders** on page 230.

Pieced by Patricia Knoechel
Quilted by Amie Potter
45" x 64"

Summer

American Beauty

Eleanor's quilt gives the illusion of peering through a kaleidoscope with shades of blue, green, pink and white. Fussy cut roses adorn the small quarter circles. The green lattice makes "window panes" and adds the right balance to the wallhanging while the border provides a lovely frame.

138

Summer Porch

In her "fat quarter friendly" scrappy quilt, Teresa selected lovely summer shades of pink, blue, and green and accented them with cool, refreshing white lattice and outside border.

Pink Lemonade

Teresa's fussy cut rose buds for the center squares, and soft green chain on a creamy white background cool even the hottest day. Her choice of rosy pink border followed by a wide border stripe add the perfect frame for her quilt.

American Beauty Wallhanging

Traditionally called Rocky Mountain or New York Beauty, this pattern dates from 1860-1870. The block was also named Lady Liberty because the points in the block are similar to the crown on the Statue of Liberty, constructed in 1865. This pattern is usually paper pieced, but American Beauty is made with Quilt in a Day's method of fusible applique. If you prefer sharp points, stick with paper piecing. But if paper piecing is a mystery to you, try this easy method.

Plan your quilting time. The best way to enjoy this pattern is in three sessions. Cut and sew the pieces in the first session, just before your favorite TV show. Take all sewn pieces and applique tools to your easy chair, turn on a bright floor lamp, and then trim and turn to your hearts content, as your TV drama drones on. In the third session, fuse and stitch down the "beauties".

Background Square
Large Quarter Circle
Small Quarter Circle

Crown

Lattice

Cornerstone

First Border

Second Border

Pieced by Eleanor Burns
Quilted by Bette Rhodaback
37" x 37"

Fabric Selection

Select sixteen fat quarters that coordinate in a variety of light, medium, and dark prints in varying scales, and colors. Use different prints as well. For balance, select eight light to medium, and eight dark.

Trace your patterns onto light-weight non-woven fusible interfacing. Do not confuse this product with paper backed fusible web. Interfacing printed with the patterns is also available.

If you can't find fat eighths, buy ¼ yd cuts. For a contemporary look, tightly woven Batiks work well.

Summer Fat Quarters from "Through the Seasons"

Fusible Interfacing   2⅓ yds
   (11) 7" strips cut into
   (32) 7" squares or
One Panel Printed Fusible Interfacing

Supplies

Applique Pressing Sheet
Fat Drinking Straw
Ball Point Bodkin
Slender Stiletto
Tweezers
Sharp 5" - 6" Trimming
   Scissors
Invisible Thread
Wooden Iron
Fine Point Permanent
   Marking Pen
Glue-Baste-It™ Temporary
   basting glue by Roxanne
   Products

Finished Block Size 6½"

Darks	Eight Dark Fat Eighths or ¼ yd Cuts Cut (3) 7" squares from each
Mediums	Eight Medium Fat Eighths or ¼ yd Cuts Cut (3) 7" squares from each
Cornerstones	⅛ yd (9) 1½" squares
Lattice	¼ yd (5) 1½" strips cut into (24) 1½" x 7" strips
Stripe	1¼ yds Cut (4) 3½" lengthwise strips
or First Border and	¼ yd (4) 1½" strips
Second Border	½ yd (4) 3½" strips
Binding	½ yd (4) 3" strips
Backing	1⅛ yds
Batting	45" x 45"

Tracing Patterns

If printed fusible interfacing is not available, trace your own patterns.

1. Find patterns for Circle and Crown in back of book on Pattern Sheet. Trace patterns on template plastic, and cut out.

2. Make two stacks of 7" fusible interfacing squares with sixteen in each stack. **Turn interfacing smooth side up.**

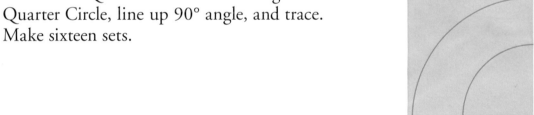

3. Place Large Quarter Circle in corner of 7" fusible interfacing square. Trace around quarter circle with permanent marking pen.

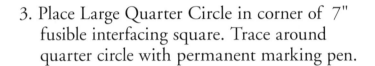

4. Place Small Quarter Circle inside Large Quarter Circle, line up 90° angle, and trace. Make sixteen sets.

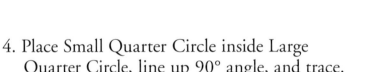

5. Trace sixteen Crowns on **smooth side** of fusible interfacing.

6. If using printed interfacing, cut apart on straight lines.

Sewing and Turning Pieces

1. Make three equal stacks of 7" squares of print fabric. Place sixteen in each stack, right side up.

 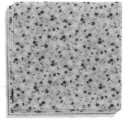 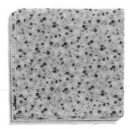 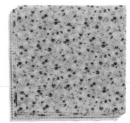

Large and Small Quarter Circles   *Crowns*   *Background Squares*

2. Take first stack of 7" print squares. Place rough, fusible side of Quarter Circles against right side of print squares. Pin.

3. Place open toe applique foot on sewing machine. If possible, lighten pressure on presser foot. Use needle down.

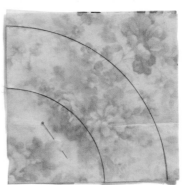

4. Sew on Large and Small Quarter Circle lines with 18 stitches to the inch, or 1.8 stitch length on computerized machine.

Sew on quarter circle lines.

5. Take out pins. Trim ⅛" from Large Quarter Circle.

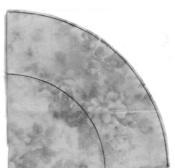

Trim ⅛" from Large Quarter Circle.

6. Trim ⅛" away from outside edge of Small Quarter Circle.

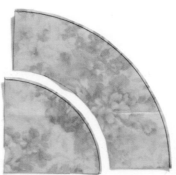

Trim ⅛" from Small Quarter Circle.

7. Turn right side out. With your fingers, turn fusible interfacing under, and crease edges with fingernails.

8. From right side, press edges with wooden iron, or press on applique pressing sheet.

9. Make a total of sixteen Large Quarter Circles and sixteen Small Quarter Circles.

Make a total of 16 sets.

10. Place rough, fusible side of Crowns against right side of print squares in second stack. Pin.

11. Sew on lines with 18 stitches to the inch, or 1.8 stitch length on computerized machine. Pivot with needle down. Sew only peaks. To make sharp points, take two stitches straight across peaks and valleys. Do not stitch on curved bottom.

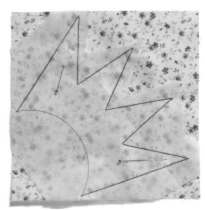

Leave curved bottom open.

12. Trim ⅛" from lines. Trim straight across tops of peaks. Clip to stitching on inside valleys.

13. Make a total of sixteen Crowns.

Clip to stitching. Be careful not to cut threads.

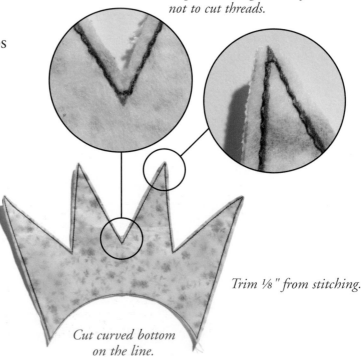

Trim ⅛" from stitching.

Cut curved bottom on the line.

14. Insert straw into point. Push straw against fabric.

Insert straw into point.

15. Place ball of bodkin on fabric stretched over straw, and gently push fabric into straw about 1" with bodkin. Remove straw and bodkin. Insert straw in second peak and repeat. Continue until all peaks are turned.

16. Gently push out points from inside with ball point bodkin or small crochet hook.

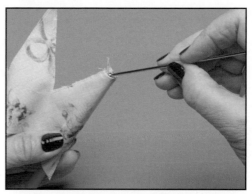

Gently push fabric into straw about 1" with bodkin. Remove straw and bodkin.

17. From right side, insert tip of stiletto into fabric, and gently pull out peak. Be careful not to break stitches and fray fabric. If you do fray fabric, glue raw edges under with Glue-Baste-It.

    Be patient. Insert stiletto and "pick" out point five or more times, until point is only slightly rounded.

Gently pull out peaks.

18. From right side, push fabric over interfacing edge with wooden iron or press on applique pressing sheet.

19. Carefully press from open bottom toward peaks.

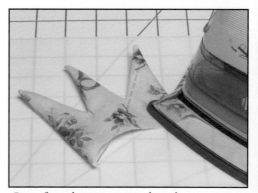

Press from bottom toward peaks.

Fusing Parts to Background

1. Lay out last stack of sixteen 7" Background squares.

2. Arrange sixteen contrasting Large Quarter Circles on squares.

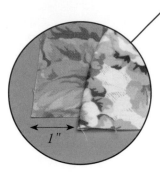

On dark 7" squares, place light to medium Large Quarter Circles.

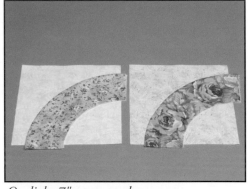

On light 7" squares, place dark Large Quarter Circles.

3. Place one at a time on applique pressing sheet.

4. Position large quarter circle 1" in on two edges.

5. Fuse in place with steam.

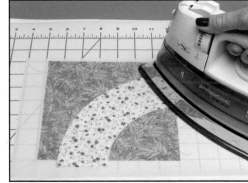

Fuse 1" in on two sides. Use measurements on pressing mat.

6. Turn square wrong side up. Trim edges even with square.

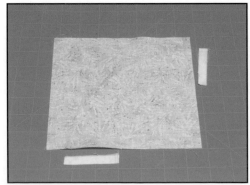

Trim from wrong side.

7. Assembly-line sew blind hem stitch or applique stitch by machine on top edge with matching or invisible thread.

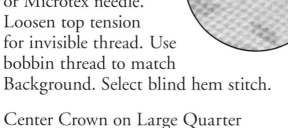

Take straight stitches on Background, and narrow "bite" into Quarter Circles.

- Use small #70 needle or Microtex needle. Loosen top tension for invisible thread. Use bobbin thread to match Background. Select blind hem stitch.

8. Center Crown on Large Quarter Circle. Position with points touching top of circle, and ¼" in on two sides. Fuse in place.

9. Trim Crown even with 7" Background square from wrong side.

Touch points to top of quarter circle. Use tweezers to position points.

10. Place Small Quarter Circle on block, lining up 90° angles. Fuse in place.

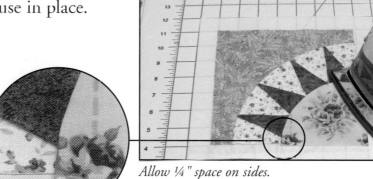

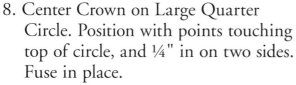

Allow ¼" space on sides.

11. Sew down Crown and Small Quarter Circles with blind hem stitch. If interfacing is showing, roll under with stiletto, and hold down before stitching.

Optional: Sew down when machine quilting.

Sewing Blocks with Lattice and Cornerstones.

1. Lay out blocks in rows, four down and four across.

2. Place 1½" Lattice and 1½" Cornerstones between blocks.

3. Flip second vertical row right sides together to first vertical row.

4. Stack from bottom up with top Lattice on top of stack.

5. Assembly-line sew. Stretch or ease each block to fit the Lattice as you sew. Do not clip connecting threads.

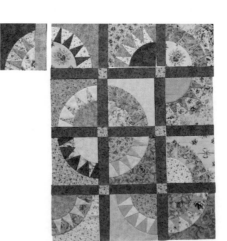

6. Open vertical rows one and two.

7. Stack third vertical row. Flip pieces in third vertical row right sides together to pieces in second vertical row. Assembly-line sew. Do not clip connecting threads.

8. Repeat with remaining vertical rows.

Sewing Horizontal Rows

1. Flip top horizontal row right sides together to second horizontal row. Stretch or case blocks and Lattice to meet, and sew.

2. At Cornerstones, where pieces are joined by threads, match seams carefully. Push seams toward Lattice for locking seams.

3. Continue sewing all horizontal rows.

4. Press from wrong side. Press from right side.

5. Turn to **Adding Borders** on page 230.

6. Quilting Suggestions: Blind hem stitch or stitch in the ditch along the Crowns. Quilt ¼" inside Small Quarter Circle, and ¼" outside Large Quarter Circle.

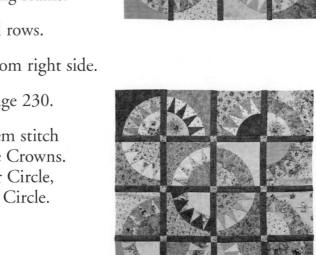

Liberty Garden

Jill and Mackie teamed up to create this original design based on the American Beauty pattern. They used the applique method from *Applique in a Day* and "Baskets & Bows", page 130 for the flowers, leaves, and vines. The border is a delightful sampler that adds interest to the quilt.

*Pieced by Jill Heers
and Mackie
Quilted by Janna Mitchell
53" x 40"*

American Beauty

Bette shows off her collection of batiks in this striking example of "American Beauty." The firm, crisp texture of batiks make them perfect for applique. Bette chose to leave out the Lattice and Cornerstones.

*Pieced and quilted by
Bette Rhodaback
37" x 37"*

New York Beauty

Eleanor created this Scrappy American Beauty pattern true to the time period, with fabrics that are reproduction Civil War prints.

Pieced by Eleanor Burns
Quilted by Teresa Varnes
38" x 38"

Purple Majesty

Carolyn Villars selected vibrant pink and rich purple hand dyed batiks to create her high contrast American Beauty.

Pieced and quilted
by Carolyn Villars
38" x 38"

Pink Lemonade Quilt

Pink Lemonade is a **One Block Repeat** quilt set together with Lattice and Cornerstones. There are two basic patches, the **Four-Patch** and the **Chevron**. The Chevron is made by combining two Flying Geese patches. Wallhanging and Lap sizes are made with 1½" x 3" finished size Flying Geese patches for a 9" block. The Twin, Full/Queen and King uses 3" x 6" finished size Flying Geese patches for an 18" block. The center of the block is ideal for fussy cuts.

The **Chain** connecting the blocks is simply a Cornerstone in the same fabric as the Four-Patch. The Chain also extends into the Borders by adding Cornerstones to all four corners of the First Border.

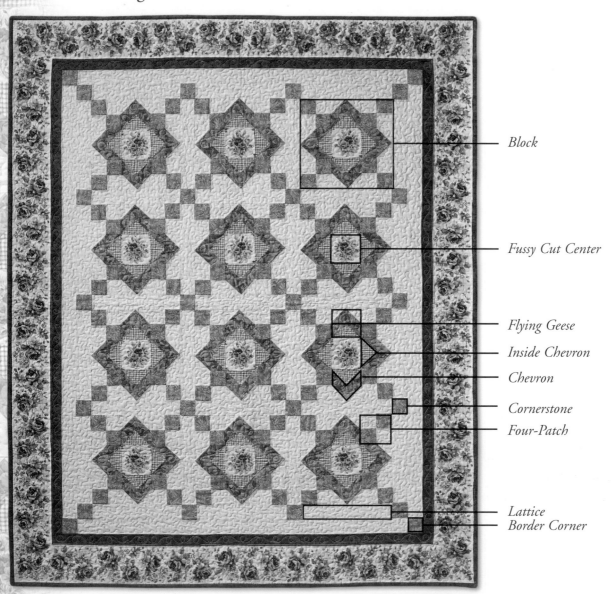

Block

Fussy Cut Center

Flying Geese

Inside Chevron

Chevron

Cornerstone

Four-Patch

Lattice
Border Corner

Pieced by Teresa Varnes
Quilted by Janna Mitchell
46" x 56"

Fabric Selection

1169-07

Multi-color Print

Choose a multi-color print fabric suitable for fussy cutting centers, either 3½" or 6½". From this piece, select coordinating fabrics for Four-Patches, Cornerstones and Chevrons. Consider repeating this fabric in the Third Border.

1167-01

Inside Chevron

Select a small scale print or plaid for around fussy cut centers. This fabric could be similar in value to the Background, but also have a little bit of color to help blend all fabrics together.

1164-01

Chevrons

Select a medium to large scale fabric that appears solid from a distance. Multi-colored prints do not work well in this part of the block because points are lost if the fabric blends into the Background. This fabric can also be repeated in the Second Border.

1170-40

Four-Patches and Cornerstones

A monochromatic fabric that appears solid from a distance works well. It should also contrast with the Chevron fabric to distinguish one from the other.

1170-07

Background

Select a tone on tone fabric that sets off all the other fabrics.

Supplies

3" x 6" Flying Geese Ruler
4" x 14" Ruler
3½" Fussy Cut Ruler
   (Wallhanging and Lap)
6½" Fussy Cut Ruler
   (Twin, Full/Queen, and King)

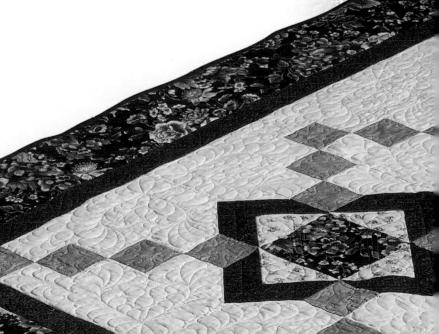

Pink Lemonade Yardage Chart

Wallhanging/Lap
Finished Block Size 9"

Twin/Queen/King
Finished Block Size 18"

		Wallhanging Nine 9" Blocks 41" x 41"	Lap Twelve 9" Blocks 50" x 60"
Background		1¼ yds	1½ yds
	Four-Patch	(4) 2" strips	(5) 2" strips
	Flying Geese	(2) 6" strips cut into (9) 6" squares	(2) 6" strips cut into (12) 6" squares
	Lattice	(6) 2" strips	(8) 2" strips
	First Border	(4) 2" strips	(6) 2" strips
Chain Fabric		⅜ yd	½ yd
	Four-Patch	(4) 2" strips	(5) 2" strips
	Cornerstones	(1) 2" strip cut into (20) 2" squares	(2) 2" strips cut into (24) 2" squares
Chevrons		⅔ yd	¾ yd
	Flying Geese	(2) 6" strips cut into (9) 6" squares	(2) 6" strips cut into (12) 6" squares
	Flying Geese	(1) 4½" strip cut into (9) 4½" squares	(2) 4½" strips cut into (12) 4½" squares
Inside Chevron		¼ yd	⅓ yd
	Flying Geese	(1) 4½" strip cut into (9) 4½" squares	(2) 4½" strips cut into (12) 4½" squares
Center Square		½ yd	½ yd
	or Fussy Cut	(1) 3½" strip cut into (9) 3½" squares	(1) 3½" strip cut into (12) 3½" squares
Second Border		⅔ yd	⅜ yd
		(5) 4" strips	(6) 2" strips
Third Border		_____	1 yd
		_____	(6) 5½" strips
Binding		½ yd	⅝ yd
		(5) 3" strips	(6) 3" strips
Backing		2¾ yds	3¼ yds
Batting		47" x 47"	55" x 66"

Measurements are based on 42" wide fabric.

Twin	Queen	King
Eight 18" Blocks	Twelve 18" Blocks	Sixteen 18" Blocks
67" x 106"	88" x 106"	106" x 106"
3¼ yds	4⅛ yds	5⅓ yds
(7) 3½" strips	(8) 3½" strips	(13) 3½" strips
(2) 9" strips cut into (8) 9" squares	(3) 9" strips cut into (12) 9" squares	(4) 9" strips cut into (16) 9" squares
(11) 3½" strips	(16) 3½" strips	(20) 3½" strips
(8) 3½" strips	(9) 3½" strips	(10) 3½" strips
1 yd	1¼ yds	1¾ yds
(7) 3½" strips	(8) 3½" strips	(13) 3½" strips
(2) 3½" strips cut into (19) 3½" squares	(3) 3½" strips cut into (24) 3½" squares	(3) 3½" strips cut into (29) 3½" squares
1⅛ yds	1½ yds	2 yds
(2) 9" strips cut into (8) 9" squares	(3) 9" strips cut into (12) 9" squares	(4) 9" strips cut into (16) 9" squares
(2) 7½" strips cut into (8) 7½" squares	(3) 7½" strips cut into (12) 7½" squares	(4) 7½" strips cut into (16) 7½" squares
¾ yd	1 yd	1½ yds
(2) 7½" strips cut into (8) 7½" squares	(3) 7½" strips cut into (12) 7½" squares	(4) 7½" strips cut into (16) 7½" squares
¾ yd	1 yd	1½ yds
(2) 6½" strips cut into (8) 6½" squares	(2) 6½" strips cut into (12) 6½" squares	(3) 6½" strips cut into (16) 6½" squares
⅝ yd	¾ yd	⅞ yd
(8) 2 ½" strips	(9) 2 ½" strips	(10) 2 ½" strips
1⅞ yds	2 yds	2⅜ yds
(9) 6 ½" strips	(10) 6 ½" strips	(12) 6 ½" strips
⅞ yd	1 yd	1⅛ yds
(9) 3" strips	(11) 3" strips	(12) 3" strips
6½ yds	8¼ yds	9¾ yds
75" x 114"	96" x 114"	114" x 114"

■ Making Four-Patches

Check your ¼" seam by sewing a test set of strips.

1. Cut Four-Patch 2" and 3½" strips for Background and Chain in half.

2. Place this many Background and Chain half strips in each stack. Sew strips right sides together. Use an accurate ¼" seam.

Number of Half Strips	
Wallhanging	8
Lap	10
Twin	14
Full/Queen	16
King	26

Use 2" strips for Wallhanging and Lap. Use 3½" strips for larger quilts.

3. Set seams with Chain fabric on top, open and press toward Chain.

Wallhanging and Lap width should measure 3½". Larger quilts width should measure 6½".

4. Place Chain fabric right sides together to Background fabric on cutting mat. Lock seams. Line up strips with grid.

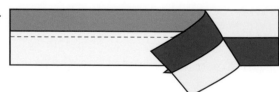

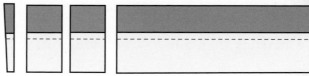

5. Square left end. Cut pairs from each strip set. Stack on spare ruler and carry to sewing area.

Number of Pairs to Cut

Wallhanging	36
Lap	48
Twin	32
Full/Queen	48
King	64

Cut 2" pairs for Wallhanging and Lap. Cut 3½" pairs for larger quilts.

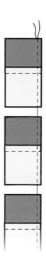

6. Matching outside edges and center seam, assembly-line sew. Use stiletto to hold outside edges together and seams flat.

7. Repeat with all pieces for Four-Patches.

8. **With Chain Fabric on left of unopened patch,** set seams, open and press.

Press as instructed so patches lock together.

9. Turn over and check from wrong side.

Making Chevrons

Chevrons are made by combining two different sets of Flying Geese patches.

Wallhanging, Lap	
Inside Chevron	4½" squares
Chevron	6" squares

Twin, Full/Queen, King	
Inside Chevron	7½" squares
Chevron	9" squares

Wallhanging, Lap	
Chevron	4½" squares
Background	6" squares

Twin, Full/Queen, King	
Chevron	7½" squares
Background	9" squares

1. Place smaller squares right sides together and centered on larger squares.

Number of Squares	
Wallhanging	9
Lap	12
Twin	8
Full/Queen	12
King	16

Number of Squares	
Wallhanging	9
Lap	12
Twin	8
Full/Queen	12
King	16

2. Place ruler on squares so ruler touches all four corners. Draw a diagonal line across squares. Pin away from the line.

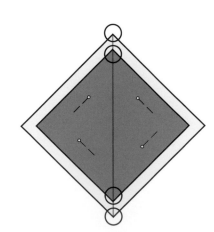

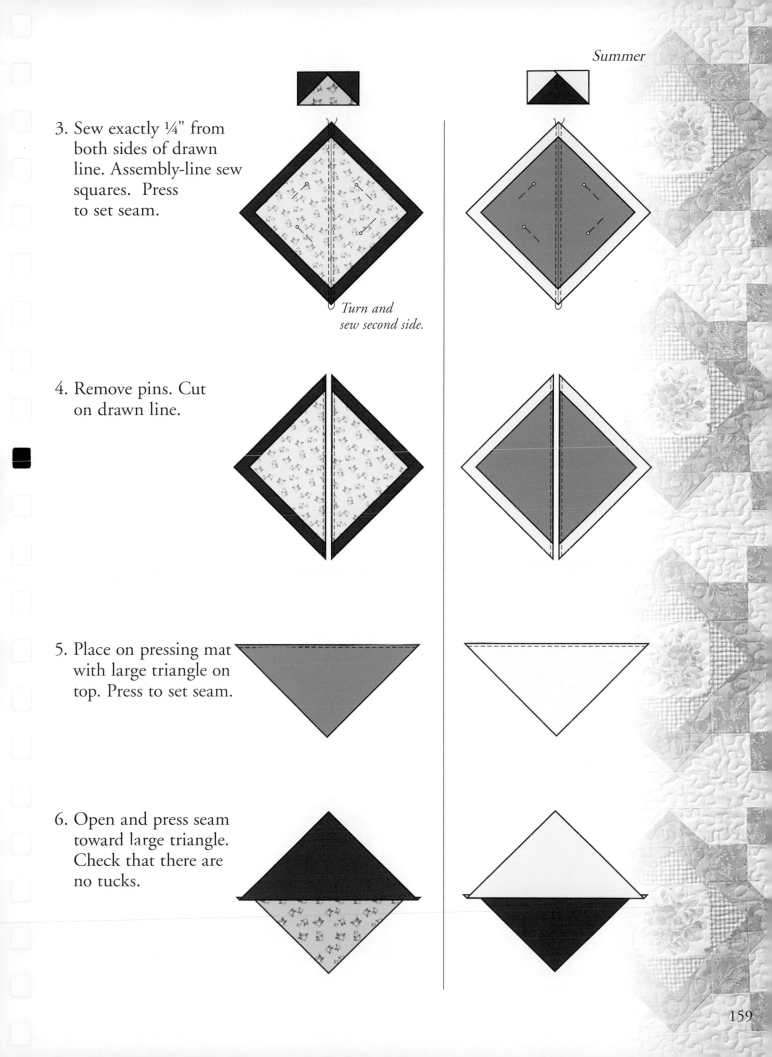

3. Sew exactly ¼" from both sides of drawn line. Assembly-line sew squares. Press to set seam.

Turn and sew second side.

4. Remove pins. Cut on drawn line.

5. Place on pressing mat with large triangle on top. Press to set seam.

6. Open and press seam toward large triangle. Check that there are no tucks.

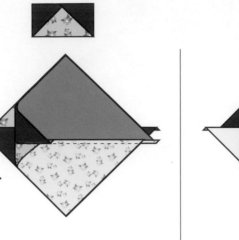

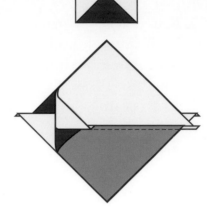

7. Place pieces right sides together so opposite fabrics touch. Seams are parallel with each other.

8. Match up outside edges. Notice gap between seams. **The seams do not lock.**

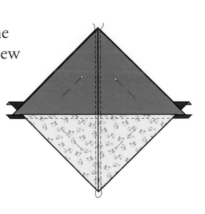

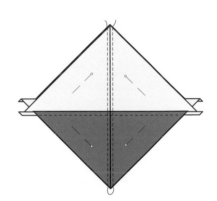

9. Draw a diagonal line across seams. Pin. Sew ¼" from both sides of drawn line. Hold seams flat with stiletto so seams do not flip. Press to set seams.

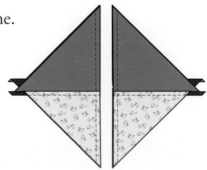

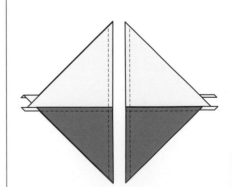

10. Cut on drawn line.

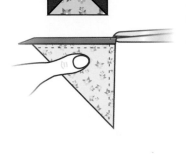

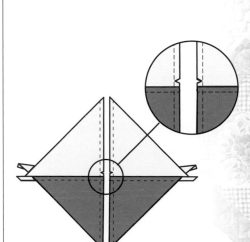

11. Fold in half and clip almost to the stitching. Now the seam allowance can be pressed away from the triangle.

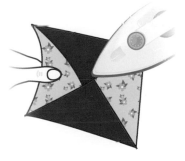

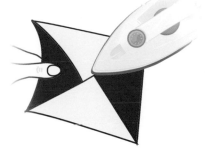

12. From the right side, press into one triangle. Turn and press into second triangle.

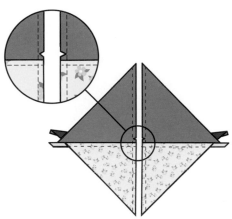

13. Turn over and press on wrong side. At clipped seam, fabric is pressed away from triangle.

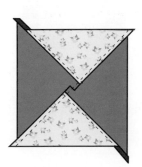

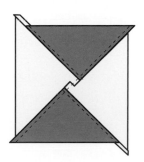

Squaring Up with 3" x 6" Flying Geese Ruler

Wallhanging and Lap

Put Invisigrip on underside of ruler.

Square to 2" x 3½" for 1½" x 3" Finished Geese.

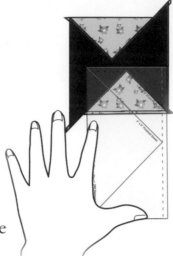
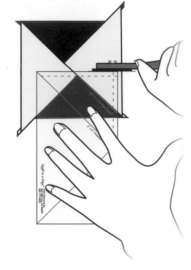

1. Line up the ruler's red lines on the 45° sewn lines. Line up red dotted straight line with peak of triangle for ¼" seam allowance. Cut block in half to separate into two patches.

2. Hold ruler securely on fabric so it does not shift while cutting. Trim off excess fabric on right.

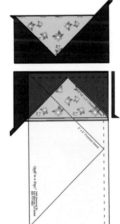
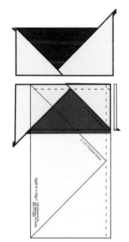

Square to 2" x 3½" for 1½" x 3" Finished Geese.

Square to 2" x 3½" for 1½" x 3" Finished Geese.

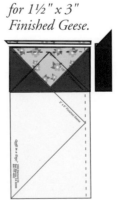
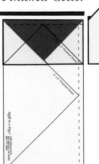

3. Turn patch around. Do not turn ruler. Trim off excess fabric on right and top.

4. Repeat with second half.

Twin, Full/Queen and King

Square to 3½" x 6½" for 3" x 6" Finished Geese.

1. Place patch on small cutting mat or revolving mat.

2. Line up green lines on 45° sewn lines. Line up green dotted straight line with peak of triangle for ¼" seam allowance. Cut block in half to separate patches.

3. Trim off excess on all four sides. Turn mat around while trimming.

Put Invisigrip on underside of ruler.

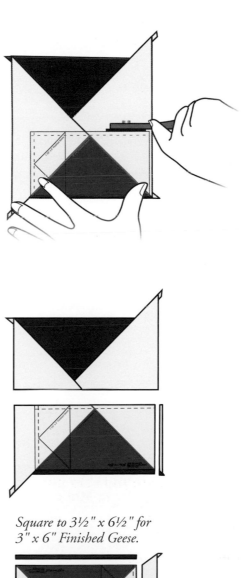

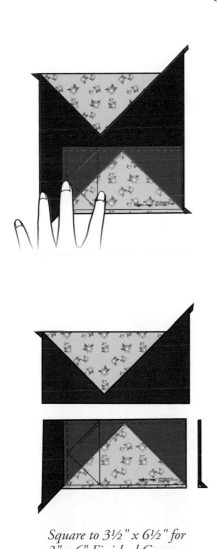

Square to 3½" x 6½" for 3" x 6" Finished Geese.

Square to 3½" x 6½" for 3" x 6" Finished Geese.

Sewing Block Together

1. Lay out the two different Flying Geese patches to make a Chevron.

Number of Chevrons

Wallhanging	36
Lap	48
Twin	32
Full/Queen	48
King	64

2. Assembly-line sew.

3. Set seam and press away from Flying Geese.

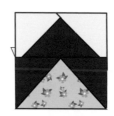

4. Lay out block. Turn patches as illustrated.

5. Flip middle vertical row patches to patches on left.

Number of Blocks to Make

Wallhanging	9
Lap	12
Twin	8
Full/Queen	12
King	16

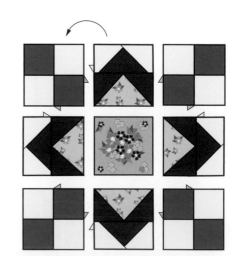

Lay out patches for locking seams.

6. Matching outside edges and locking seams, assembly-line sew.

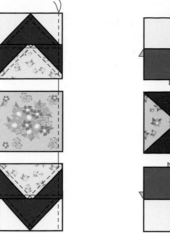

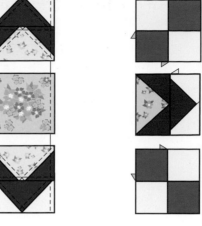

7. Open first two rows.

8. Flip right vertical row to middle row.

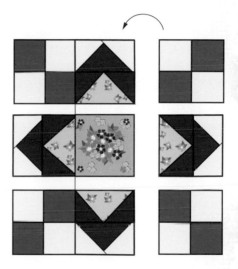

9. Assembly-line sew.

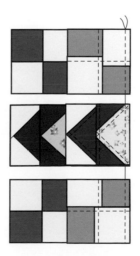

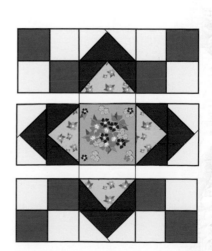

10. Turn block one quarter turn. Flip row on right to middle row.

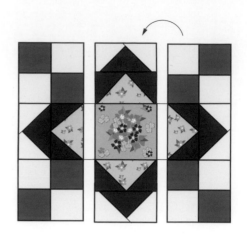

11. Press seams away from Chevrons and lock together. Assembly-line sew.

12. Sew last row, pressing seams away from Chevrons.

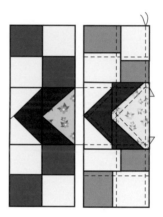

13. Press final seams away from center row.

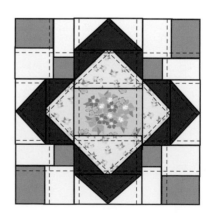

Laying Out Quilt Top

1. Measure pressed block. Block should be approximately 9½" for Wallhanging and Lap sizes and 18½" for Twin, Full/Queen and King. Block size should be consistent.

2. Cut Lattice strips the same length as block.

Number of Lattice	
Wallhanging	24
Lap	31
Twin	22
Full/Queen	31
King	40

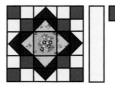

Cut 2" strips for Wallhanging and Lap.
Cut 3½" strips for larger quilts.

3. Lay out blocks, leaving space for Lattice and Cornerstones.

Number of Blocks	
Wallhanging	3 x 3
Lap	3 x 4
Twin	2 x 4
Full/Queen	3 x 4
King	4 x 4

4. Place Lattice strips and Cornerstones between blocks.

5. Assembly-line sew all vertical rows. See page 148 for **Sewing Blocks with Lattice and Cornerstones.**

6. Assembly-line sew remaining rows, pressing seams toward Lattice.

3 x 4 Example of Lap in 9½" Blocks and
3 x 4 Full/Queen in 18½" Blocks

7. Measure quilt top.

8. **Background First Border:** For larger quilts, remove selvages and assembly-line sew into longer pieces.

9. Cut four First Border strips the same size as your quilt top.

10. Pin Border to sides. Sew from quilt side with Border on the bottom. Press seams toward Border.

Cut First Border exactly the same size as sides.

11. Sew a Cornerstone to each end of top and bottom Border. Press seams toward Border.

12. Pin top and bottom Border to quilt. Sew and press seams toward Border.

13. Add remaining Borders. Turn to **Adding Borders** on page 230.

Roses for Mom

The pretty fussy cut center square sets the tone for Sue's lovely quilt. She drew the shades of her large-scale outside border into her quilt by using the pink and rose tones in her blocks and sage green chain. Delightful!

Pieced by Sue Bouchard
Quilted by Amie Potter
44" x 44"

A Walk in the Park

For drama, Sue selected a large-scale print with black background for her border. She fussy cut her center squares from the same print and used a soft creamy background with green chains. The first border of burgundy provides the perfect frame on her quilt.

Pieced by Sue Bouchard
Quilted by Carol Selepec
88" x 108"

169

Summer Porch Quilt

Summer Porch Quilt is as fresh as white wicker rockers covered with comfy colorful pillows on a wrap-around porch. It's easy to make from a **One Block Repeat**, made oversized and squared to perfection! Dig into your pastel stash, or treat yourself to some new prints in summertime florals. Quick as a bug you cut squares on the diagonal, and sew them back together with a refreshing light Lattice.

For a bold, contemporary look, check out the Stained Glass Quilt made by Patricia Knoechel on page 185. Her blocks are bright Batiks and prints with a black Lattice, set together in a symmetrical design.

It's a summer fireworks show of color!

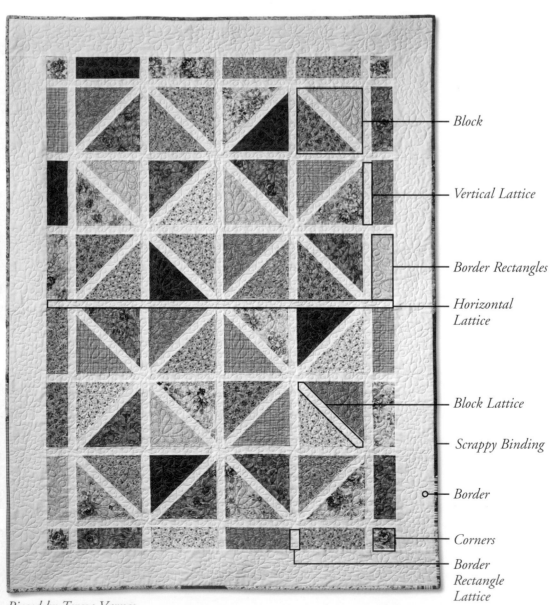

— Block

— Vertical Lattice

— Border Rectangles

— Horizontal Lattice

— Block Lattice

— Scrappy Binding

— Border

— Corners

— Border Rectangle Lattice

Pieced by Teresa Varnes
Quilted by Janna Mitchell
49" x 64"

Selecting Fabric

Scrappy Blocks

Choose an assortment of light medium to dark print fabrics in a variety of scales and values from your stash, fat quarters, or ¼ yard cuts. The more variety in fabrics, the easier it is to arrange blocks without same fabrics next to each other.

Coordinating fabrics from one fabric line work well in this quilt. Look for bundles of fat quarters designed to go together.

Summer Fat Quarters from "Through the Seasons"

Stained Glass Look

For variety, select black or very dark purple for Lattice.

Combine with a variety of bright intense fabrics, such as Batiks, or mottled fabrics. Lay out blocks in symmetrical designs.

Lattice

Choose a solid looking tone on tone fabric that contrasts with the prints.

Supplies

9½" Square Up Ruler
12½" Square Up Ruler
18" Shape Cut Plus
Glow-Line™ Tape
1" Tape
Stiletto

Summer Porch Yardage Chart

Finished Block Size 7½"		Wallhanging 40" x 40" 4 x 4, 16 Blocks	Lap 46" x 62" 4 x 6, 24 Blocks
Stash			
	Blocks	(16) 8" squares	(24) 8" squares
	Border Rectangles	(16) 3" x 8"	(20) 3" x 8"
	Scrappy Binding	(8) 3" half strips	(12) 3" half strips
	Corners	(4) 3" squares	(4) 3" squares
Or Fat Quarters or ¼ yd Cuts		8 fat quarters or ¼ yd cuts Cut from each	12 fat quarters or ¼ yd cuts Cut from each
	Blocks	(2) 8" squares	(2) 8" squares
	Border Rectangles	(16) 3" x 8"	(20) 3" x 8"
	Scrappy Binding	(1) 3" half strip	(1) 3" half strip
	Corners	(4) 3" squares from any print	(4) 3" squares from any print
Lattice		¾ yd	1⅛ yds
	Horizontal Lattice	(5) 1½" strips Set aside	(7) 1½" strips Set aside
	Block Lattice	(11) 1½" strips cut into (16) 1½" x 11½" strips	(15) 1½" strips cut into (24) 1½" x 11½" strips
	Vertical Lattice	(20) 1½" x 8" strips	(30) 1½" x 8" strips
	Border Rectangle Lattice	(10) 1½" x 3" strips	(10) 1½" x 3" strips
Border		———	1 yd (6) 5" strips
Binding If not Scrappy		⅜ yd (4) 3" strips	¾ yd (6) 3" strips
Backing		1¼ yds	3 yds
Batting		48" x 48"	52" x 68"

Yardage is based on 42" wide fabric.
Cutting Instructions on pages 174 - 176.

Twin	Full/Queen	King
76" x 108"	92" x 108"	108" x 108"
6 x 10, 60 Blocks	8 x 10, 80 Blocks	10 x 10, 100 Blocks
(60) 8" squares	(80) 8" squares	(100) 8" squares
(32) 5" x 8"	(36) 5" x 8"	(40) 5" x 8"
(19) 3" half strips	(20) 3" half strips	(22) 3" half strips
(4) 5" squares	(4) 5" squares	(4) 5" squares
16 fat quarters or ¼ yd cuts Cut from each	**20 fat quarters or ¼ yd cuts** Cut from each	**25 fat quarters or ¼ yd cuts** Cut from each
(4) 8" squares	(4) 8" squares	(4) 8" squares
(32) 5" x 8"	(36) 5" x 8"	(40) 5" x 8"
———	———	———
(4) 5" squares Cut later	(4) 5" squares Cut later	(4) 5" squares Cut later
2⅓ yds	**3 yds**	**3¾ yds**
(17) 1½" strips Set aside	(22) 1½" strips Set aside	(25) 1½" strips Set aside
(35) 1½" strips cut into (60) 1½" x 11½" strips (70) 1½" x 8" strips (14) 1½" x 5" strips	(45) 1½" strips cut into (80) 1½" x 11½" strips (90) 1½" x 8" strips (18) 1½" x 5" strips	(57) 1½" strips cut into (100) 1½" x 11½" strips (110) 1½" x 8" strips (22) 1½" x 5" strips
2¾ yds (9) 10" strips	**3 yds** (10) 10" strips	**3¼ yds** (11) 10" strips
1 yd (10) 3" strips	**1 yd** (10) 3" strips	**1 yd** (11) 3" strips
6½ yds	**10 yds**	**10 yds**
82" x 114"	98" x 114"	114" x 114"

Layer Cutting Fat Quarters

1. Press and stack up to five fat quarters, right sides up. Line up cut straight edges.

2. Cut according to your quilt size. If necessary, **skimp into selvages** so you still have 21" of fabric.

3. Set aside 3" x 8" Border Rectangles and 3" Scrappy Binding strips for Wallhanging and Lap.

Wallhanging and Lap

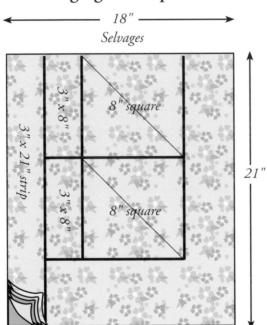

Twin, Full/Queen and King

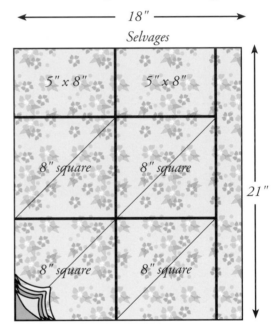

Cut from each fat quarter

Scrappy Binding	(1) 3" x 21"
Border Rectangles	(2) 3" x 8"
Blocks	(2) 8" squares cut on one diagonal

Cut from each fat quarter

Blocks	(4) 8" squares cut on one diagonal
Border Rectangles	(2) 5" x 8"

4. Layer cut 8" squares on one diagonal.

5. Divide triangles into two equal stacks.

Layer Cutting ¼ Yard Cuts

1. Open on fold and press.

2. Stack up to five ¼ yard cuts, right side up. Line up selvages on left edge, and **trim selvages sparingly**, especially on ¼ yds for larger quilts.

3. Cut according to your quilt size.

4. Set Border Rectangles and Scrappy Binding for Wallhanging and Lap aside.

Wallhanging and Lap

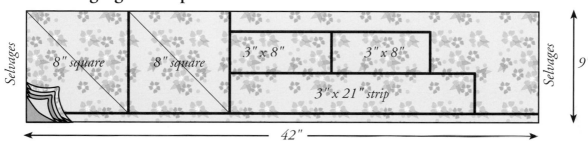

Cut from each 1/4 yard

Blocks	(2) 8" squares cut on one diagonal
Border Rectangles	(2) 3" x 8"
Scrappy Binding	(1) 3" half strip

Twin, Full/Queen and King

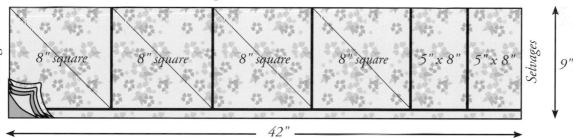

Trim selvages sparingly. Measurements are based on a 42" width. If you can't get the second 5" x 8" rectangle, replace it with another fabric.

Cut from each 1/4 yard

Blocks	(4) 8" squares cut on one diagonal
Border Rectangles	(2) 5" x 8"

5. Layer cut 8" squares on one diagonal.

6. Divide triangles into two equal stacks.

Cutting Lattice Strips

1. **Horizontal Lattice:**
   Cut selvage to selvage 1½"
   Lattice strips according
   to your size yardage chart.

2. Mark and set aside.

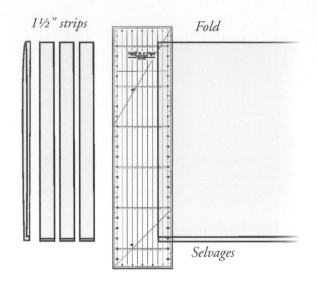

1½" strips

Fold

Selvages

3. Line up selvage edges on
   remaining fabric, and trim
   selvages with 6" x 24" Ruler.

4. **Block and Vertical Lattice:**
   Cut selvage to selvage 1½"
   Lattice strips according to
   your size yardage chart.

5. Leave 1½" strips laying
   on cutting mat.

6. Cut 1½" strips into 11½"
   Block Lattice and 8" Vertical
   Lattice with 12½" Square Up
   Ruler or Shape Cut, according
   to your size yardage chart.

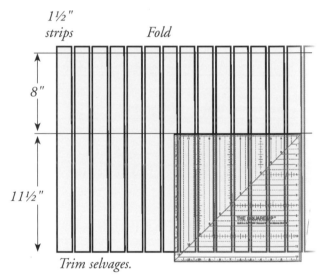

1½" strips *Fold*

8"

11½"

Trim selvages.

7. **Border Rectangle Lattice:**
   After cutting the total number of 11½" and 8" strips
   needed, cut leftovers into
   1½" x 3" for Wallhanging
   and Lap, or 1½" x 5" strips
   for larger sizes.

8. Stack strips right sides up.

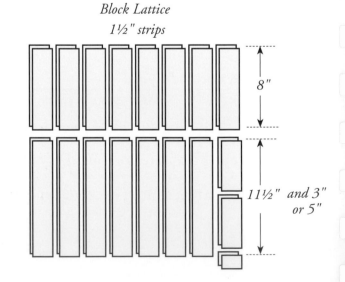

Block Lattice
1½" strips

8"

11½" and 3"
or 5"

Sewing Blocks

1. Place stack of 1½" x 11½" Block Lattice to right of one stack of Triangles.

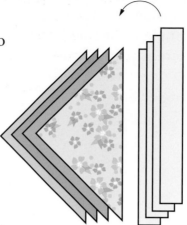

2. Flip Lattice right sides together to Triangle. Match tip of Triangle with top of strip.

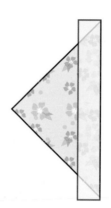

3. Assembly-line sew with ¼" seam. **Do not use a generous ¼" seam.**

4. Clip apart.

5. Set seam with triangle on top. Open and press seam toward Triangle.

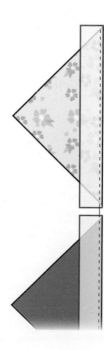

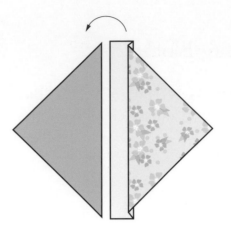

6. Place second stack of Triangles to left of Lattice/Triangle. Flip Lattice/Triangle right sides together to **different print Triangle**, lining up top edges. Make sure tips on two triangles line up.

7. Assembly-line sew with Triangle on bottom so bias on Triangle does not stretch.

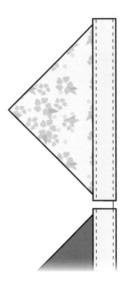

8. Set seam with Triangle on top. Open, and press toward Triangle.

9. Clip apart.

10. Check pressing from wrong side.

Number of Blocks

Wallhanging	16
Lap	24
Twin	60
Full/Queen	80
King	100

Squaring Block to 8"

1. Place Block on cutting mat.

2. Use 9½" Square Up Ruler. Place ruler's diagonal line down center of Lattice.

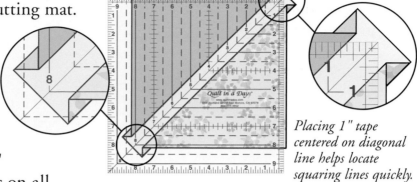

3. Center ruler at 8" with excess fabric on all four sides.

Placing 1" tape centered on diagonal line helps locate squaring lines quickly.

You may need to square your block to a smaller consistent size such as 7⅞". Trim back 8" Vertical Lattice to same measurement. Place Glow-Line Tape on measurement to help locate squaring lines quickly.

4. Trim top and right sides of Block.

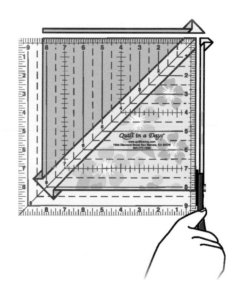

5. Turn Block. **Do not turn ruler.**

6. Place 8" squaring lines on freshly cut edges.

7. Trim remaining two sides.

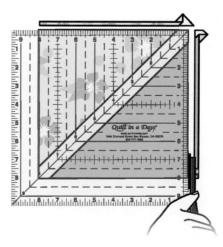

Sewing Top Together

1. Working on floor or design wall, lay out four different Blocks in diamond shape.

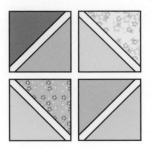

2. Continue working in groups of four, laying out Blocks in diamond shape. Be careful not to repeat same fabrics side by side.

3. Evenly space heavy contrasting fabrics. Notice spacing of the dark blue fabric.

Number of Blocks

Wallhanging	4 x 4
Lap	4 x 6
Twin	6 x 10
Full/Queen	8 x 10
King	10 x 10

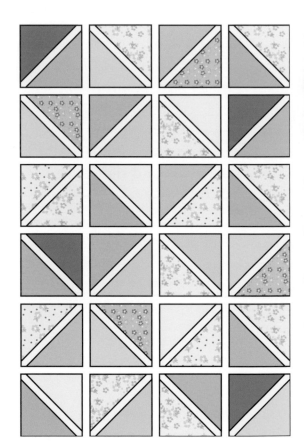

Example of Lap   *4 x 6*

4. Place Border Rectangles around outside edge.

5. If you haven't already, cut four Corner Squares from left over Border Rectangles, and place in corners.

Size of Corner Squares

Wallhanging/ Lap	3" squares
Twin/Full/ Queen/King	5" squares

6. To avoid mixing Blocks later, write numbers on small labels equal to your number of rows.

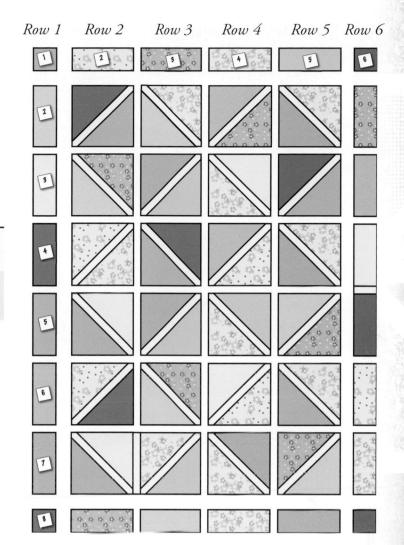

7. Stick labels on top center patch of top row and far left row, beginning with Row One in upper left Corner Square.

8. Stack all patches into vertical rows from top to bottom, keeping top patch on top of each stack. **Set far right row aside.**

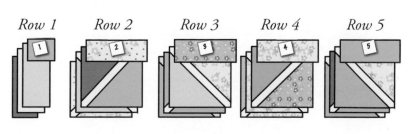

Set aside.

181

9. Place stacks of Border Rectangle Lattice and Vertical Lattice on right side of numbered rows: 1½" x 3" for Wallhanging and Lap, or 1½" x 5" for larger sizes, and 1½" x 8".

   Do not place Lattice with far right row.

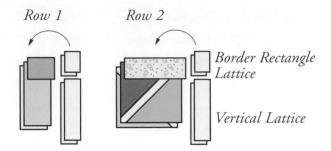

Border Rectangle Lattice

Vertical Lattice

10. Flip appropriate size Lattice right sides together to patch. Assembly-line sew all vertical rows.

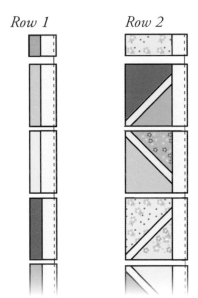

11. Clip patches apart. Stack in rows in order.

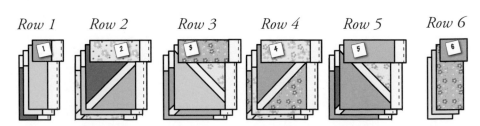

12. Set seam with Lattice on top, being careful to avoid label. Open, and press seam toward Lattice.

13. Assembly-line sew Blocks in vertical Rows One and Two together. Clip apart and stack in order.

Row 1   *Row 2*

14. Continue adding vertical rows, including last row.

15. Clip connecting threads. Remove labels.

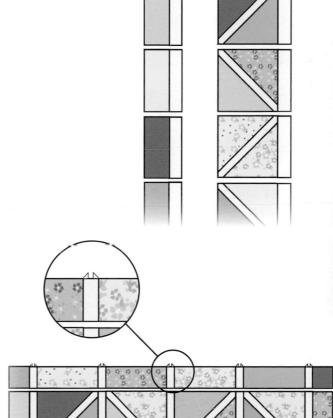

16. Press seams toward Lattice.

17. Carefully lay out sewn rows.

18. If necessary, sliver trim and straighten edges of rows.

Adding 1½" Horizontal Lattice Strips

1. Trim selvage edges on 1½" Lattice strips.

2. **Wallhanging and Lap:** It is not necessary to piece Lattice strips.

   Twin, Full/Queen, King: Piece together 1½" selvage to selvage strips.

Number of Strip Sets	
Twin	(11) sets of 1½ strips each
Full/Queen	(11) sets of 2 strips each
King	(11) sets of 2¼ strips each

40"   40"   10"   *Example of King 2¼ strips*

3. Place 1½" Lattice strip at bottom of each row, **except bottom row**.

4. Sew 1½" strips to bottom of all rows. Sew with Blocks on top, pushing seams as pressed. Trim Lattice.

5. Set seam with Lattice on top, open, and press toward Lattice.

6. Place each row back in layout as completed.

7. Sew rows together, lining up Vertical Lattice strips.

8. Set seam with Lattice on top, open, and press toward Lattice.

9. Turn to **Adding Borders** on page 230.

Scrappy Binding

1. Piece 3" half strips together, and press seams open.

2. Follow **Binding** instructions on page 235.

Stained Glass Look

Pieced by Patricia Knoechel
Quilted by Amie Potter
57" x 57"

Stained Glass Yardage

Lattice	1½ yds cut into
	(31) 1½" strips
Horizontal Lattice	(11) 1½" strips set aside
Block Lattice	(36) 1½" x 11½"
Vertical Lattice	(42) 1½" x 8"
Border Lattice	(14) 1½" x 3"
¼ yd of 10 different batiks and prints	
Three dark blue	Cut each into (4) 8" squares, (3) 3" x 8"
Three medium green	Cut each into (4) 8" squares, (3) 3" x 8"
Three light blue/green	Cut each into (4) 8" squares, (3) 3" x 8"
One red	Cut into (4) 8" squares, (4) 3" squares
Binding	⅝ yd (6) 3" strips
Backing	3¾ yds
Batting	64" x 64"

1. Cut 8" squares on one diagonal.

2. Referring to photo, lay out triangles for blocks on design wall from center out. Follow placement of colors. For interest, mix up blues, greens, and lights.

3. Sew top together, placing 3" x 8" rectangles around outside edge, and 3" red squares in corners.

Autumn

Harvest Tablerunner

The holidays would not be complete without the historic Horn of Plenty. With fall leaves, grapes, a sunflower, squash, and a pumpkin, Aiko's tablerunner display is a lot to be thankful for. To add dimension, bits of batting were used in the pumpkin and grapes.

Buckeye Quilt

Using 5" squares, Teresa made this charming scrappy quilt, perfect for cool fall evenings. She selected green and brown fabrics for borders to frame her quilt. This is the perfect project to use up those bits of fabric that are just to good to toss out!

Country Lanes Quilt

Sue created this lovely quilt that features a large scale print in the border and solid blocks. Her chains in "read-as-solid" prints of green and tan add just the right touch to the background.

Harvest Tablerunner

Grace your autumn table with an elegant, traditional Horn of Plenty. Appliqued Leaves falling from the Cornucopia are brightened with a robust Pumpkin and country Sunflower.

There are two different styles: one with striped and mitered Borders with Cornucopia centered on each end, and one without Borders and with fall foliage tumbling over the edges.

The Tablerunner can be lengthened or shortened to fit any table by cutting the Background to fit and lengthening side Borders.

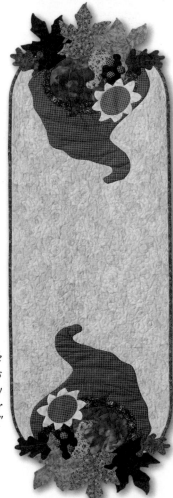

Maple Leaf

Oak Leaf

Pumpkin

Cornucopia

Background

Stripe Border

Oval

Sunflower

Grape Cluster

Squash

*Handwork
by Aiko Rogers
Quilted by
Amie Potter
16" x 48"*

*Border by Teresa Varnes
Applique by Eleanor Burns
Handwork by Aiko Rogers
Machine Quilting by Janna Mitchell
21" x 78"*

Fabric Selection

Background
Select a medium to large scale tone on tone floral in a fabric that contrasts with the Cornucopia and fall applique.

1172-73

Border
Select a 3½" stripe or print that contrasts with the Background, and compliments the colors of the fall foliage. Corners on the stripes are mitered.

1171-79

Applique
Select a check or basket weave for the Cornucopia, and a contrasting fabric for the Oval inside the Cornucopia. Select fabrics true to the colors of the Leaves, Grapes, Pumpkin with Stem, and Squash.

Fusible Interfacing
Use light to medium weight non-woven fusible interfacing to turn under raw edges of applique. Do not confuse this product with paper backed fusible web. Interfacing printed with the patterns is also available.

Supplies

Template Plastic
Fine Point Permanent Marking Pen
Applique Pressing Sheet
Fat Drinking Straw
Ball Point Bodkin
Stiletto
Hemostat
Sharp 5"-6" Trimming Scissors
Invisible Thread
Wooden Iron
Glue-Baste-It™ Temporary Basting Glue by Roxanne Products
6" x 24" Ruler with 45° line

Harvest Tablerunner Yardage Chart

		Tablerunner with Striped Border 21" x 78"		Oval Tablerunner 16" x 48"
Background		2 yds		1½ yds
Stripe Border		1¾ yds (4) 3½" lengthwise strips		_____
or Print Border		¾ yd (6) 3½" strips		_____
Cornucopia	Brown Check	½ yd (2) 13" x 15"	Green Check	½ yd (2) 13" x 15"
Oval	Green	¼ yd (2) 7" x 10½"	Purple	¼ yd (2) 7" x 10½"
		Stash or ¼ yd cuts of each		Stash or ¼ yd cuts of each
Pumpkin	Orange	(2) 7" squares		(2) 7" squares
Maple Leaves	Green, Purple, Rust	(2) 7" squares of each		(4) 7" squares of each
Pumpkin Stem	Green	(2) 3½" squares		(2) 3½" squares
Squash	Rust	(2) 3½" x 6"		(2) 3½" x 6"
Sunflower	Petals	(2) 5" x 6"		(2) 5" x 6"
	Center	(2) 4" x 3"		(2) 4" x 3"
Oak Leaves	Deep Rust	(2) 3½" x 6"		(4) 3½" x 6"
	Light Rust	(2) 3½" x 6"		(4) 3½" x 6"
Grapes	Dark Purple	(1) 2½" strip		(1) 2½" strip
	Checked Purple	(2) 2½" strips		(2) 2½" strips
Non-Woven Fusible Interfacing	Cut pieces same size as applique pieces except Grapes.	1¾ yds	Cut pieces same size as applique pieces except Grapes and Leaves.	1½ yds
Binding		¾ yd (6) 2¾" strips		½ yd (6) 2" bias strips (see page 197)
Backing		2¼ yds		_____
Batting	100% Cotton	25" x 90"		22" x 72"
	Polyester Stuffing	Handful		Handful

Tracing Patterns for Both Tablerunners

If printed fusible interfacing is not available, follow these directions for tracing your own patterns.

1. Find patterns on Pattern Sheet. Trace patterns on template plastic, and cut out.

2. Cut interfacing into pieces the same size as applique pieces.

3. Turn non-woven fusible interfacing **smooth side up**.

4. Center and trace patterns on interfacing with permanent marking pen.

5. Place rough, fusible side of interfacing against right side of appropriate fabric, and pin.

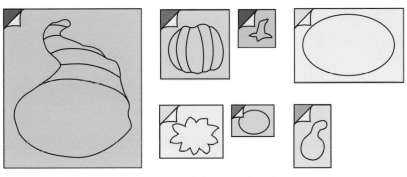

Make two of each.

Tablerunner with Striped Border

1. Trace Leaves on interfacing, including veins.

2. Place fusible side of interfacing against right side of fabric, and pin.

Make two of each.

Oval Tablerunner

1. Trace Leaves on wrong side of one piece of fabric.

2. Place two pieces of fabric right sides together, and pin.

Make two of each.

Sewing and Turning Pieces

1. Place open toe applique foot on sewing machine. If possible, lighten pressure on presser foot.

2. Sew on lines with 18 stitches to the inch, or 1.8 stitch length on computerized machine. Use needle down, and overlap ending and beginning stitches. Do not sew on inside lines.

3. Trim ⅛" from lines.

4. **Interfacing:** Cut a small slit in center.
   Fabric Backed Leaves: Cut a small slit in one fabric near bottom of leaf.

5. Turn right side out with straw and ball point bodkin. Press edges with wooden iron. See pages 53-54.

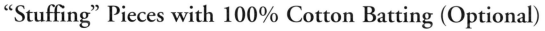

"Stuffing" Pieces with 100% Cotton Batting (Optional)

For added dimension, Cornucopia, Leaves on interfacing, Squash, Pumpkins, and tops of Sunflowers can be "stuffed" with 100% cotton batting, and lines stitched from the back side. However, pieces become thick for later quilting. Do not stuff fabric Leaves.

1. Place turned applique piece on top of 100% cotton batting.

2. Cut batting piece to exact size of applique piece.

3. Insert batting through opening of interfacing with hemostat. Manipulate batting to outside edges.

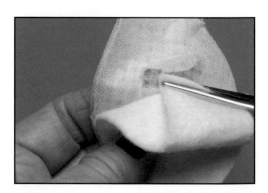

4. **Leaves with Interfacing:** Sew on vein lines from interfacing side with thread matching fabric.
   Fabric Leaves: Sew vein lines with thread matching fabrics.

   If you prefer, leave out the batting and sew vein lines when quilting whole tablerunner.

Making Grapes

1. Find 2" circle on Pattern Sheet, trace on template plastic, and cut out.

Make fourteen dark grapes.

2. Trace fourteen 2" circles on dark purple, and six 2" circles on checked purple, and cut out.

Make six light grapes.

3. Thread hand sewing needle with double strand of matching thread, and knot.

4. Run a gathering stitch around the outside edge. Stuff with grape size ball of stuffing, and draw tight.

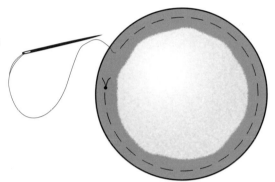

5. Set Aside. Grapes are stitched to Cornucopia last.

Making Background for Pointed Tablerunner

Tablerunner finished size with Borders is 21" x 78".

1. Cut Background lengthwise into 16" x 72" piece.

   Measure length and width of your table. Lengthen or shorten to fit by cutting the Background to your desired size. If Tablerunner is too wide, shrink patterns 25%.

2. Fold in half lengthwise into 8" x 72" piece. Place fold across top.

3. Place 6" x 24" Ruler's 45° line across top on fold, and trim ends into point.

4. Repeat on opposite end of Tablerunner.

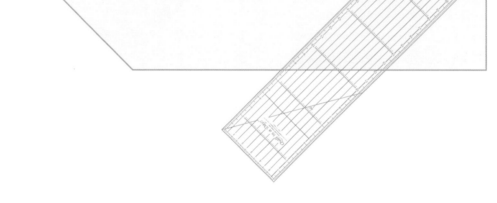

5. Pin and sew Borders on long sides. Press seams toward Borders.

6. Trim side Borders following lines of point.

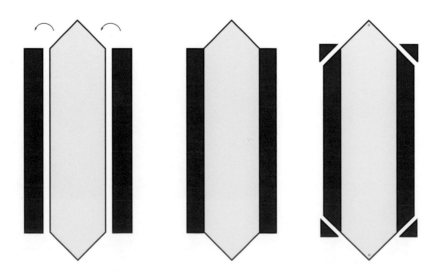

Making Mitered Corners on Border

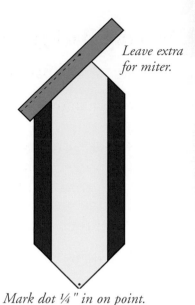

Leave extra for miter.

1. Mark dot and place pin ¼" in on both points.

2. Cut four 21" strips from remaining Border strips.

3. Pin strip and sew, stopping on ¼" marks. Pull strip out of the way of ¼" marks. Repeat with second strip.

4. See directions for mitering beginning on page 227.

Mark dot ¼" in on point.

Fusing Parts to Background

1. Place Cornucopia on Background 2" in from sides, and 10½" in from point. Center Oval inside Cornucopia. Fuse in place with steam. Press from wrong side.

2. Stitch around outside edges of Oval and Cornucopia with blind hem stitch or applique stitch.

3. Position large Maple leaves and fuse in place. Stitch around outside edges.

4. Position small Oak leaves, fuse in place, and stitch around outside edges.

5. Position Pumpkin with Stem, Squash, and Sunflower with center, fuse in place, and stitch around outside edges.

6. Stitch Grapes to Cornucopia.

7. Turn to **Layering Your Quilt** on page 231.

Making Background for Oval Tablerunner

1. Cut 1½ yds Background fabric in half lengthwise on fold.

2. Layer 100% cotton Batting between two pieces of Background, and safety pin.

3. Machine quilt with stippling or cross hatch stitching.

4. Trim to 16" wide.

5. Place 10" or 10½" plate on each corner, and trace around plate. Trim.

6. Bind with 2" bias strips, and stitch in place.

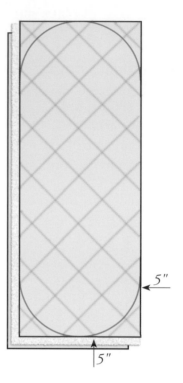

5"

5"

7. Center Cornucopia on Background next to Binding. Center Oval inside Cornucopia. Fuse in place with steam, or pin in place. Stitch around outside edges with blind hem stitch or applique stitch.

8. Position large Maple Leaves hanging over edges, and pin in place. Tuck Small Oak Leaves around Maple Leaves, pin in place, and sew down.

9. Position Pumpkin with Stem, Squash, and Sunflower with center, fuse or pin in place, and stitch around outside edges.

10. Stitch Grapes in place.

Making Bias Binding

1. Cut ½ yd into 16"
   selvage to selvage strip.

2. Line up 45° line on
   6" x 24" Ruler with left
   edge of 16" strip.

3. Cut on diagonal.
   Fabric from triangle to
   left of ruler can be cut
   into bias strips as well.

4. Move ruler over 2"
   from diagonal cut.
   Cut again.

5. Cut six 2" bias strips.

6. Piece bias strips together on angle to outside measurement of your tablerunner.

7. Press diagonal seams open.

8. Follow Binding instructions on page 235,
   easing Binding around curves.

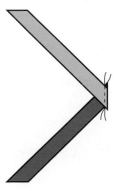

Buckeye Beauty Wallhanging

The Wallhanging is made of **Four-Patch Blocks** in medium tones, and **Pieced Triangle Square Blocks** in dark tones. Four of these sets of patches sewn together make a Star Block. With the addition of one Background, and First and Second Borders, this Wallhanging is quick and easy to make, especially with a pack of thirty-two 5" squares from a fabric manufacturer.

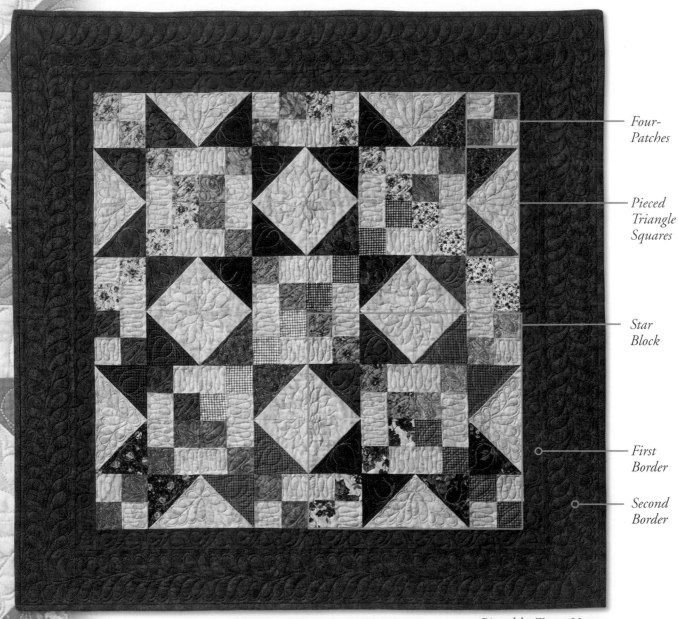

Four-Patches

Pieced Triangle Squares

Star Block

First Border

Second Border

Pieced by Teresa Varnes
Quilted by Janna Mitchell
41" x 41"

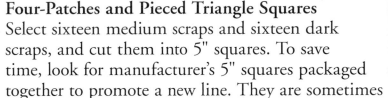

Fabric Selection

5" squares from
"Through the Seasons"

Four-Patches and Pieced Triangle Squares
Select sixteen medium scraps and sixteen dark scraps, and cut them into 5" squares. To save time, look for manufacturer's 5" squares packaged together to promote a new line. They are sometimes referred to as nickel square packs.

If the 5" squares are from a new line, purchase additional matching fabric for Borders to tie scrappy looking blocks together. Select a tone on tone for the narrow First Border, and a multi-colored print for the second Border.

1164-73

Background
Select a tone on tone, textured fabric to offset the Four-Patches and Pieced Triangle Squares. This fabric should enhance the scrappy fabrics by providing contrast.

Finished Size Block 15"	Wallhanging 41" x 41" 2 x 2
Darks	(16) different 5" squares
Mediums	(16) different 5" squares
Background	⅔ yd (4) 5" strips cut into (32) 5" squares
First Border	⅓ yd (4) 2" strips
Second Border	⅝ yd (4) 4½" strips
Binding	½ yd (5) 3" strips
Backing	1¼ yds
Batting	48" x 48"

Supplies

6½" Triangle Square Up Ruler
6" Square Up Ruler
6" x 12" Ruler
Rotating Mat (Optional)

Making Four-Patches

1. Pair up one 5" Background square with each of the sixteen different Medium squares.

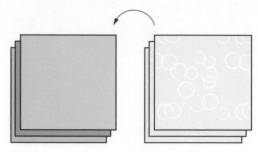

Each set of squares makes two patches.

2. Place squares right sides together. Draw a line at 2½".

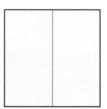

3. Sew ¼" from both sides of drawn line.

4. Set seams, and cut on drawn line.

5. Press seams toward Medium fabric.

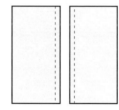

6. Place right sides together, matching Medium to Background. Seams lock together.

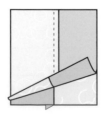

7. Turn, and draw a line at 2½".

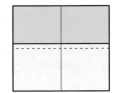

8. Sew ¼" from both sides of drawn line.

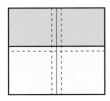

9. Set seams, and cut on drawn line. Separate into two stacks.

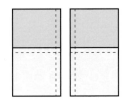

10. Open and place wrong side up on pressing mat. Press just sewn vertical seams as illustrated. Half go one way and half go the other way.

11. Flatten center to make a small Four-Patch.

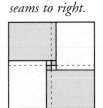

Press top vertical seams to right.

Press bottom vertical seams to left.

Press top vertical seams to left.

Press bottom vertical seams to right.

12. Using 6" Square Up Ruler, square patch to 4¼".

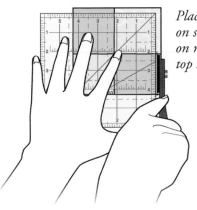

Place 2⅛" lines on seams. Trim on right and top sides.

Turn patch. Do not turn ruler. Place ruler's 4¼" lines on freshly cut edges. Trim on right and top sides. Rotating mat is very helpful.

Making Pieced Triangle Squares

1. Pair up one 5" Background square with each of the sixteen different Dark squares.

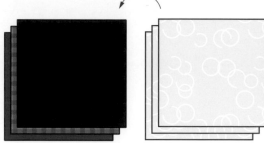

Each set of squares makes two patches.

2. Place squares right sides together. Draw one diagonal line.

3. Sew ¼" from both sides of drawn line.

4. Set seams, and cut on drawn line.

5. Using 6½" Triangle Square Up Ruler, square patch to 4¼".

6. Press seams to Dark. Trim tips.

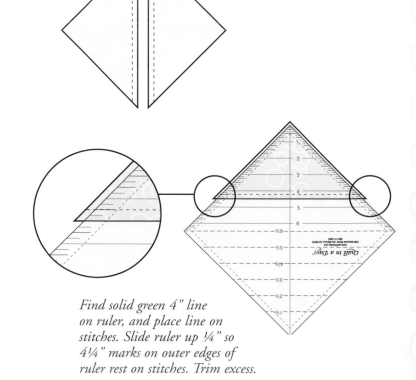

Find solid green 4" line on ruler, and place line on stitches. Slide ruler up ¼" so 4¼" marks on outer edges of ruler rest on stitches. Trim excess.

Sewing Sixteen Quarter Blocks

1. Choose two identical Four-Patches and two identical Pieced Triangle Squares for each of the sixteen blocks.

2. Lay out sixteen blocks. **Pay particular attention to seams on Four-Patches.**

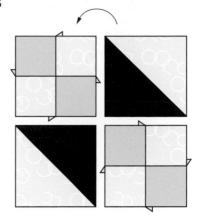

3. Flip patches on the right over patches on the left.

4. Assembly-line sew vertical row.

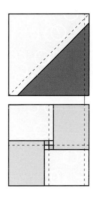

5. Clip two block sets apart.

6. Finger press seams toward Four-Patches.

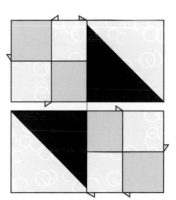

7. Turn patches 90° to the left.

8. Flip patches on right over patches on left.

9. Assembly-line sew blocks together.

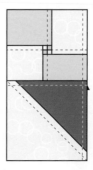

Push top seam up, and underneath seam down.

10. Clip connecting thread in middle seam. Push top vertical seam to right, and bottom vertical seam to left. Flatten center to make a little Four-Patch.

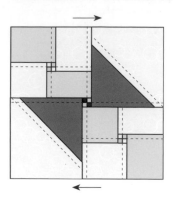 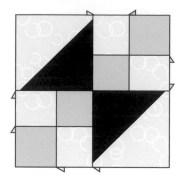

Completing Top

1. Lay out four blocks to make one Star. Turn blocks as needed so seams lock together. Pay particular attention to seams on Four-Patches.

2. Sew four blocks together into Star. Sew remaining three Stars.

3. Sew four Stars together, locking seams.

4. Turn to **Adding Borders** on page 230.

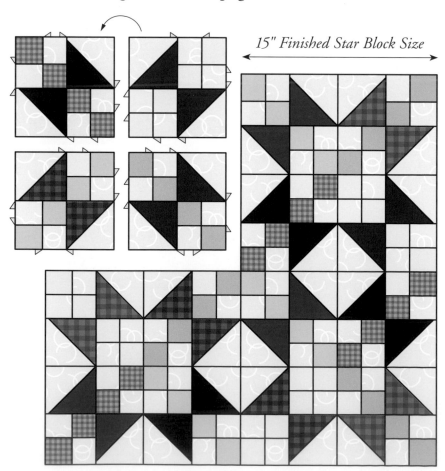

15" Finished Star Block Size

Buckeye Beauty

If you enjoyed making the Buckeye Beauty Wallhanging from a pack of thirty-two 5" squares, and want to make larger quilts, follow these simple quantities and figure your own additional fabrics.

Lap	3 packs	12 Stars	3 x 4
Twin	4 packs	15 Stars	3 x 5
Full/Queen	5 packs	20 Stars	4 x 5
King	7 packs	25 Stars	4 x 5

Pieced by Mackie
Quilted by Judy Jackson
62" x 92"

Machine Quilting

Janna Mitchell used several patterns to add dimension and interest to each area of this quilt. A curved feather pattern fills in the border. The large solid squares are enhanced with multi-pedaled flowers and leaves.

Country Lanes Quilt

This easy strip pieced quilt is made simply of two blocks, a **Chain Block**, and a **Large Scale Floral Block**. The pattern comes from alternating the two. The Chains extend to the outside edges with **Border Chain Patches** and **Corner Patches**. **Border Rectangles** from Background complete the top. Patches appear to "float" with the First Border in Background. This Background area is perfect for showing off your quilting! Repeating the Large Scale Floral in the Second Border pulls all fabrics together.

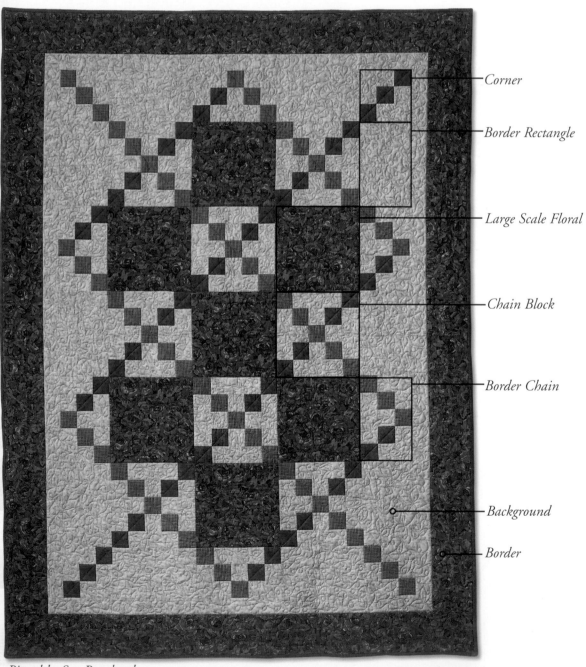

— Corner

— Border Rectangle

— Large Scale Floral

— Chain Block

— Border Chain

— Background

— Border

Pieced by Sue Bouchard
Quilted by Amie Potter
54" x 74"

Fabric Selection

Only four fabrics are used in Country Lanes! You will be "strolling" in no time!

Large Scale Floral
This quilt is perfect for showcasing your favorite multi-colored Large Scale Print!

1164-78

Chains
Select fabrics for Chain One and Chain Two in colors pulled from the Large Scale Floral. Monochromatic, or tone on tone fabrics work best flowing across the quilt. For clarity in the Chains, they must contrast with the Large Scale Floral, and each other. In this example, the brown check is Chain One and the green is Chain Two.

1167-78

1172-44

Background
Select a print with tonal texture to offset the Chains and Large Scale Floral fabrics. This fabric should enhance the other fabrics by providing a contrast base.

1172-73

Supplies

6" x 12" Ruler
12½" Square Up Ruler
4" x 14" Ruler

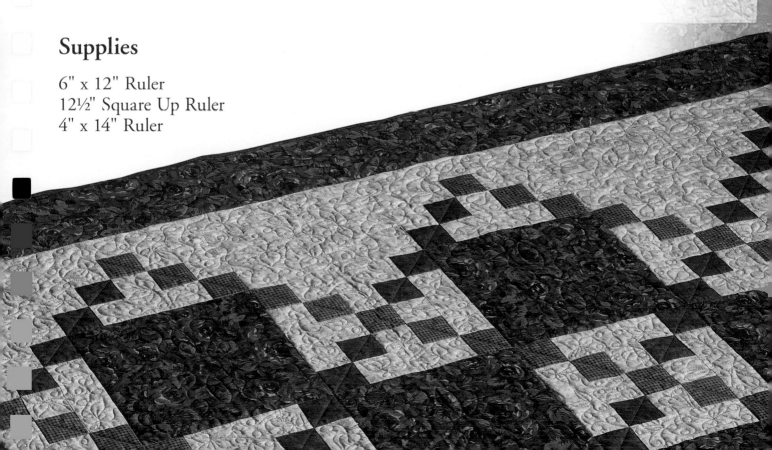

Country Lanes Yardage Chart

		Wallhanging 54" x 54" 3 x 3	Lap 56" x 76" 3 x 5
Finished Block Size 10"			
Background		2⅛ yds	2½ yds
	Chain	(7) 2½" strips Cut in half on fold	(8) 2½" strips Cut in half on fold
	Border Chains	(2) 4½" strips Cut in half on fold	(2) 4½" strips Cut in half on fold
	Chain	(2) 6½" strips Cut in half on fold	(2) 6½" strips Cut in half on fold
	Border Rectangles	(2) 6½" strips cut into (8) 6½" x 10½"	(3) 6½" strips cut into (10) 6½" x 10½"
	First Border	(5) 2½" strips	(7) 2½" strips
Chain One		½ yd	½ yd
		(5) 2½" strips Cut in half on fold	(5) 2½" strips Cut in half on fold
Chain Two		⅜ yd	⅜ yd
		(4) 2½" strips Cut in half on fold	(4) 2½" strips Cut in half on fold
Large Scale Floral		⅜ yd	⅔ yd
	Solid Squares	(1) 10½" strip cut into (4) 10½" squares	(2) 10½" strips cut into (7) 10½" squares
Second Border		⅞ yd (6) 4½" strips	1¼ yds (7) 5½" strips
Binding		⅝ yd (6) 3" strips	⅔ yd (7) 3" strips
Backing		3⅓ yds	4¾ yds
Batting		60" x 60"	64" x 84"

Measurements are based on 42" wide fabric.

Twin	Full/Queen	King
60" x 112"	92" x 112"	112" x 112"
3 x 7	5 x 7	7 x 7
3¼ yds	4¾ yds	5⅓ yds

(11) 2½" strips
   Cut in half on fold
	(16) 2½" strips
	   Cut in half on fold
		(19) 2½" strips
		   Cut in half on fold

(2) 4½" strips
   Cut in half on fold
	(3) 4½" strips
	   Cut in half on fold
		(3) 4½" strips
		   Cut in half on fold

(3) 6½" strips
   Cut in half on fold
	(4) 6½" strips
	   Cut in half on fold
		(5) 6½" strips
		   Cut in half on fold

(3) 6½" strips cut into
   (12) 6½" x 10½"
	(4) 6½" strips cut into
	   (14) 6½" x 10½"
		(4) 6½" strips cut into
		   (16) 6½" x 10½"

(8) 3½" strips	(9) 5½" strips	(11) 5½" strips
⅞ yd	1 yd	1 yd

(8) 2½" strips
   Cut in half on fold
	(11) 2½" strips
	   Cut in half on fold
		(13) 2½" strips
		   Cut in half on fold

⅝ yd	¾ yd	1 yd

(6) 2½" strips
   Cut in half on fold
	(8) 2½" strips
	   Cut in half on fold
		(10) 2½" strips
		   Cut in half on fold

1 yd	1⅝ yds	1⅞ yds

(3) 10½" strips cut into
   (10) 10½" squares
	(5) 10½" strips cut into
	   (17) 10½" squares
		(6) 10½" strips cut into
		   (24) 10½" squares

1¾ yds	3⅜ yds	3¾ yds
(9) 6½" strips	(11) 10½" strips	(12) 10½" strips
⅞ yd	1 yd	1⅛ yds
(9) 3" strips	(11) 3" strips	(12) 3" strips
6¾ yds	10 yds	10 yds
68" x 120"	100" x 120"	120" x 120"

Making Chain Blocks

Making Nine-Patches

1. Lay out 2½" half strips of Background and Chain One. Turn right side up with cut edge at top. Place this many half strips in each stack.

Number of Half Strips	
Wallhanging	1
Lap	1
Twin	2
Full/Queen	3
King	4

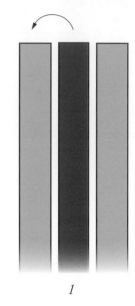

1

2. Sew strips together lengthwise.

3. Press seams away from Background.

4. Measure width of strips. They should measure approximately 6½".

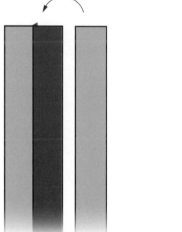

5. Cut each set into 2½" sections with ruler or Shape Cut.

Number of 2½" Sections	
Wallhanging	5
Lap	8
Twin	11
Full/Queen	18
King	25

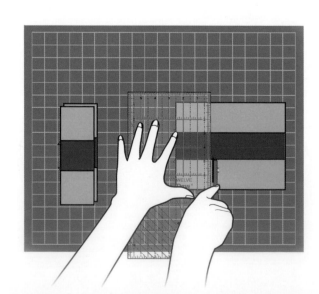

6. Lay out 2½" half strips of Chain One, Background, and Chain Two. Place this many half strips in each stack.

Number of Half Strips

Wallhanging	2
Lap	2
Twin	4
Full/Queen	5
King	7

1   *2*

7. Sew all strips together lengthwise.

8. Press seams away from Background.

9. Cut each set into 2½" sections.

Number of 2½" Sections

Wallhanging	10
Lap	16
Twin	22
Full/Queen	36
King	50

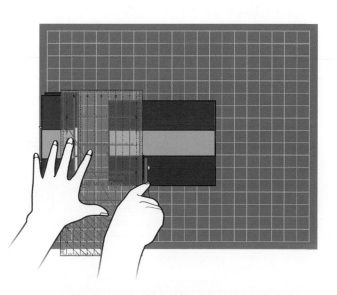

10. Lay out pieces to form a Nine-Patch.

11. Lock seams, and assembly-line sew first two sets together.

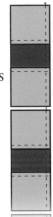

12. Assembly-line sew third set. Clip blocks apart.

13. Press seams away from middle row.

14. Measure size and record.

_____ Approx. 6½"

Approximately 6½"

Sewing Round One Sides

1. Stack Nine-Patches with Chain Two in upper left corner.

2. Place 2½" Background half strips to left of Nine-Patches.

Number of Half Strips	
Wallhanging	2
Lap	3
Twin	4
Full/Queen	6
King	8

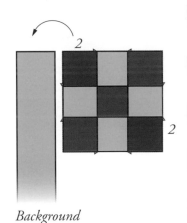

Background

3. Flip Nine-Patches right sides together to strip and assembly-line sew.

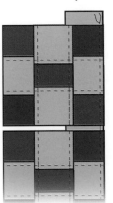

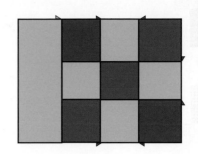

4. Cut strips even with Nine-Patches.

5. Turn over with strips on top. Set seam, open, and press seams away from Nine-Patches.

6. Stack Nine-Patches with Chain Two in upper left corner.

7. Place 2½" Background half strips to left of Nine-Patches.

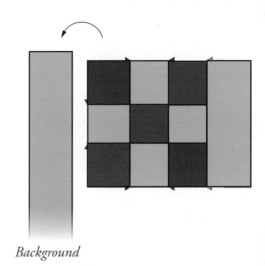

Background

Number of Half Strips	
Wallhanging	2
Lap	3
Twin	4
Full/Queen	6
King	8

8. Flip Nine-Patches right sides together to strip and assembly-line sew.

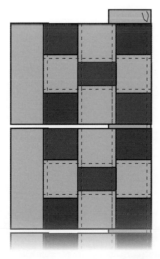

9. Cut strips even with Nine-Patches.

10. Press seams away from Nine-Patches.

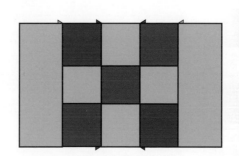

Sewing Round One Top and Bottom

Background

1. Refer to measurement of Nine-Patches on page 212. If necessary, sliver trim 6½" Background half strips to size of Nine-Patches.

6½" wide

2. Lay out 6½" Background half strips and 2½" half strips of Chain One and Chain Two. Place this many half strips in each stack. Assembly-line sew.

1   Approx. 6½"   2

Number of Half Strips

Wallhanging	2
Lap	2
Twin	4
Full/Queen	5
King	7

3. Press seams toward Background.

4. Cut 2½" sections.

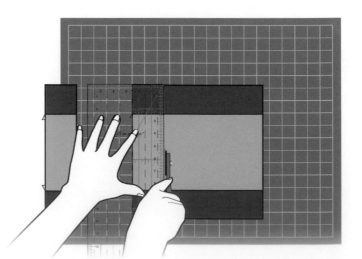

Number of 2½" Sections

Wallhanging	10
Lap	16
Twin	22
Full/Queen	36
King	50

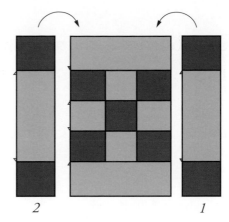

5. Assembly-line sew 2½" sections to both sides of Nine-Patches. Make sure Chains line up. Clip apart.

Optional: Pin locking seams.

6. Press seams away from Nine-Patches.

7. Measure size and record.

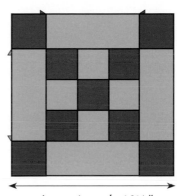

_____ Approx. 10½"

Approximately 10½"

8. Refer to measurement of block. If necessary, sliver trim 10½" Large Scale Floral strips to size of block.

9. Cut 10½" strips into 10½" squares.

Number of Squares	
Wallhanging	4
Lap	7
Twin	10
Full/Queen	17
King	24

215

Making Border Chain

Row One

1. Lay out 4½" half strips of Background and 2½" half strips of Chain One. Place the number indicated for your size in each stack.

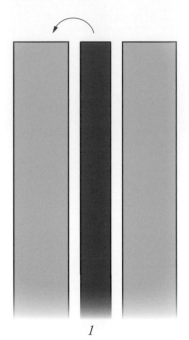

1

Number of Half Strips

Wallhanging	1
Lap	1
Twin	1
Full/Queen	2
King	2

2. Sew strips together lengthwise from cut edge. Press seams toward Background.

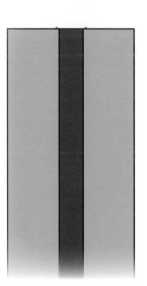

3. Cut into 2½" sections.

Number of 2½" Sections

Wallhanging	4
Lap	6
Twin	8
Full/Queen	10
King	12

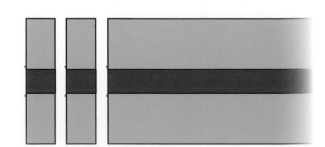

Row Two

1. Lay out 2½" half strips of Background, Chain One and Chain Two. Place this many in each stack.

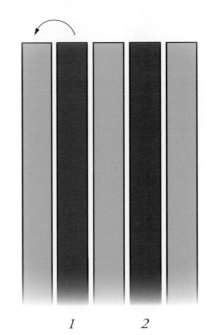

Number of Half Strips

Wallhanging	1
Lap	1
Twin	1
Full/Queen	2
King	2

2. Sew strips together lengthwise. Press seams toward Background strips.

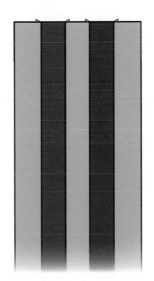

3. Cut into 2½" sections.

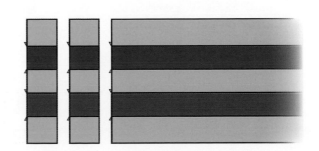

Number of 2½" Sections

Wallhanging	4
Lap	6
Twin	8
Full/Queen	10
King	12

Row Three

1. Lay out 2½" half strips of Chain One and Chain Two with 6½" half strips of Background. Place this many in each stack.

Number of Half Strips	
Wallhanging	1
Lap	1
Twin	1
Full/Queen	2
King	2

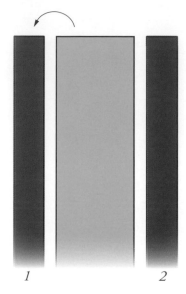

2. Sew strips together lengthwise. Press seams toward Background strips.

3. Cut into 2½" sections.

Number of 2½" Sections	
Wallhanging	4
Lap	6
Twin	8
Full/Queen	10
King	12

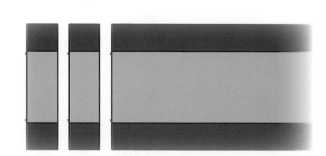

Making Side Border Chain

1. Lay out rows for Side Border Chain, lining up Chains.

Number in Each Stack	
Wallhanging	2
Lap	4
Twin	6
Full/Queen	6
King	6

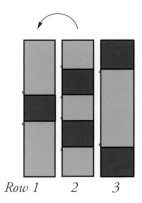

Row 1   2   3

2. Assembly-line sew.

3. Press seams toward Row One.

4. Pin together, and label.

Making Top and Bottom Border Chains

1. Lay out rows for Top and Bottom Border Chain, lining up Chains.

Number in Each Stack	
Wallhanging	2
Lap	2
Twin	2
Full/Queen	4
King	6

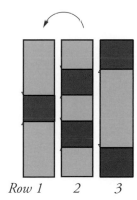

Row 1   2   3

2. Assembly-line sew.

3. Press seams toward Row One.

4. Pin together, and label.

Making Corner Patches

Each quilt has two Corner Patches from Chain One and two Corner Patches from Chain Two.

Rows One and Three

1. Sew 2½" half strips of Chain One and Chain Two with 4½" half strips Background.

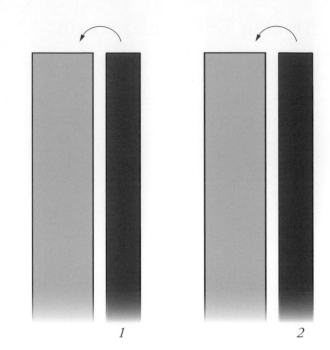

1   *2*

2. Press seams toward Background.

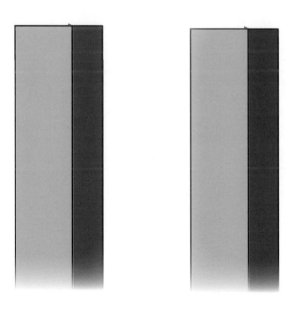

3. Cut each strip set into (4) 2½" pieces.

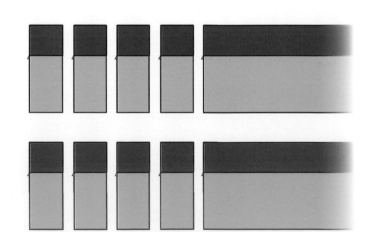

Row Two

1. Cut two 2½"
   Background half strips
   into four quarter strips
   approximately 10" long.

2. Cut half strips of Chain
   One and Chain Two
   into quarter strips. Set
   a quarter strip of each
   aside.

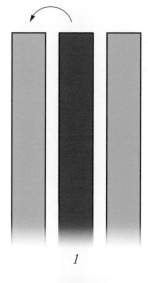

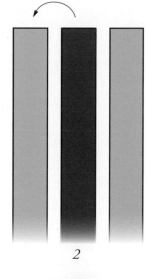

1   2

3. Assembly-line sew a
   Background strip to each
   side of Chain strip.

4. Press seams toward
   Background.

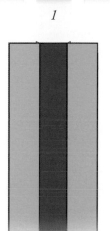

5. Cut each strip set into
   two 2½" pieces.

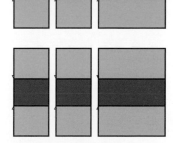

6. Lay out rows for
   Corner Patches, and
   assembly-line sew.

7. Press seams away from
   center row.

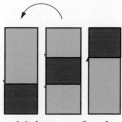

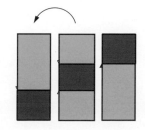

Make two of each.

Sewing Top Together

1. Lay out your selected size quilt.

2. Assembly-line sew vertical rows together. Do not clip connecting threads.

Wallhanging

Large Scale Print Squares	4
Chain Blocks	5
Rectangles	8
Side Border Patches	2
Top and Bottom Border Patches	2
Chain 1 Corner Patches	2
Chain 2 Corner Patches	2

Lap

Large Scale Print Squares	7
Chain Blocks	8
Rectangles	10
Side Border Patches	4
Top and Bottom Border Patches	2
Chain 1 Corner Patches	2
Chain 2 Corner Patches	2

Twin

Large Scale Print Squares	10
Chain Blocks	11
Rectangles	12
Side Border Patches	6
Top and Bottom Border Patches	2
Chain 1 Corner Patches	2
Chain 2 Corner Patches	2

3. Sew remaining rows, pressing seams toward Border Rectangles and Large Scale Florals.

4. Turn to **Adding Borders** on page 230.

Full/Queen

Large Scale Print Squares	17
Chain Blocks	18
Rectangles	14
Side Border Patches	6
Top and Bottom Border Patches	4
Chain 1 Corner Patches	2
Chain 2 Corner Patches	2

King

Large Scale Print Squares	24
Chain Blocks	25
Rectangles	16
Side Border Patches	6
Top and Bottom Border Patches	6
Chain 1 Corner Patches	2
Chain 2 Corner Patches	2

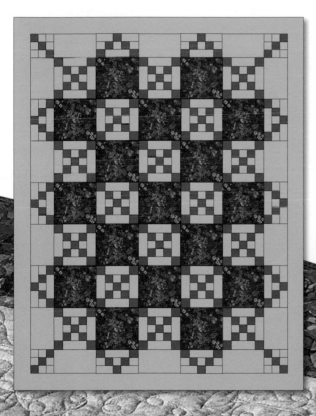

Finishing Your Quilt

Stripe Borders with Mitered Corners

1. Calculate the length of the strip. The total length includes length of the quilt, plus two times the width of the stripe, plus 6" inches at each end to match the flower or design in the corner.

2. Before cutting off end of strip, lay out the long side strips next to the quilt.

3. At a 45° angle, turn under one end of the strip to see where the seam will fall. Ideally the seam will not fall on a large flower.

4. Lay out top and bottom strips. Fold back corners to check placement. Adjust if necessary, and cut length of strips.

Position stripe with a flower at each end.

Mark dot ¼" down from top edge of quilt.

5. Flip a side strip onto the quilt. On the wrong side of the strip, mark a dot ¼" in from the top and bottom edges of the quilt. Make dots on remaining side border. Pin on dots through both layers and in middle of strip.

6. Lockstitch on dot, and sew along the line printed on the fabric.

7. Stop sewing on the dot ¼" up from the bottom edge of the quilt, and lockstitch.

8. In same manner, sew strip to opposite side of quilt.

9. Press seams toward Border.

10. Flip top and bottom strips onto quilt, and mark dots ¼" in from edge of quilt.

11. Sew top and bottom strips to quilt. Lock stitch and stop on dots. Seams will meet side strips ¼" in from edges.

Keep side seams out of the way.

Mitered Corner

1. Fold top diagonally and line up two strips right sides together.

2. Line up the diagonal line on a 12½" Square Up ruler with the outside edge of the strips. Line up the right edge of the ruler with the dot where the stitches meet.

3. Draw a sewing line from the outside edge to the dot.

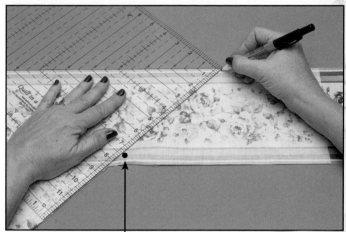

Line up the right edge of the ruler with the dot where the stitches meet.

4. Place pins at the points where the drawn line crosses the fabric line. Check pin alignment with the second strip underneath.

5. Starting at the outside edge, stitch along the drawn line to the dot, pulling pins out of the way before sewing. Lockstitch.

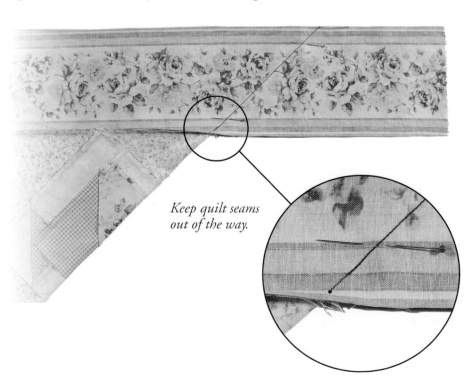

Keep quilt seams out of the way.

6. Trim seam allowance to ¼" and press seams open.

7. Miter all four corners in this manner.

Mitering from Right Side of Stripe

Try this method if your stripes are not lining up with the previous method.

1. Place corner on pressing mat. Fold top strip under diagonally, and line up two Border strips. Press diagonal crease with iron.

2. Place 12½" Square Up Ruler's 45° line on seam. Check that corner is square.

3. Pin in place. Sew from right side with blind hem stitch and invisible thread, straight stitch, or hand stitch.

4. Trim seam allowance and press open.

Adding Borders

1. Cut Border strips according to your Yardage Chart.

2. Trim selvages.

3. Lay first strip right side up. Lay second strip right sides to it. Backstitch, stitch, and backstitch again.

4. Continue assembly-line sewing all short ends together into long pieces.

5. Cut Border pieces the average length of both sides.

6. Place Border right sides together to side. Pin layers together in center, on ends, and several places between each.

7. Sew to sides.

8. Set seam with Border on top. Open and press seams toward Border.

9. Measure width. Cut Border pieces for top and bottom. Pin and sew.

10. Press seams toward Border.

11. Continue adding any remaining Borders.

Layering Your Quilt

1. If necessary, piece Backing.

2. Spread out Backing on a large table or floor area, right side down. Clamp fabric to edge of table with quilt clips, or tape Backing to the floor. Do not stretch Backing.

3. Layer Batting on Backing and pat flat.

4. With quilt right side up, center on Backing. Smooth until all layers are flat. Clamp or tape outside edges.

Safety Pinning

1. Place pin covers on 1" safety pins. Safety pin through all layers three to five inches apart. Pin away from where you plan to quilt.

2. Catch tip of pin in grooves on pinning tool, and close pins.

3. Use pinning tool to open pins when removing them. Store pins opened.

"Stitch in the Ditch" along Blocks and Borders

1. Thread your machine with matching thread or invisible thread. If you use invisible thread, loosen your top tension. Match the bobbin thread to the Backing.

2. Attach your walking foot, and lengthen the stitch to 8 to 10 stitches per inch or 3.0 on computerized machines.

3. Tightly roll quilt from one long side to center. Place hands on quilt in triangular shape, and spread seams open. Stitch in the ditch along seam lines and anchor blocks and borders.

4. Roll quilt in opposite direction, and stitch in the ditch along seam lines.

Quilting Blocks or Outline Quilting with Darning Foot

The advantage to using a darning foot to quilt is that you don't need to constantly pivot and turn a large heavy quilt as you do with a walking foot.

1. Attach darning foot to sewing machine. Drop feed dogs or cover feed dogs with a plate. No stitch length is required as you control the length. Use a fine needle and invisible or regular thread in the top and regular thread to match the bobbin. Loosen top tension if using invisible thread. Use needle down position.

2. Plan what to outline, or how to stitch around block, covering as many seams continuously as possible.

3. Place hands flat on block. Bring bobbin thread up on seam line or edge of design.

4. Lock stitch and clip thread tails. Free motion stitch around block or design. Keep top of block at top. Sew sideways and back and forth without turning quilt.

5. Lock stitch and cut threads. Continue with remaining blocks.

Marking for Free Motion Quilting

1. Select an appropriate stencil.

2. Center on area to be quilted, and trace lines with disappearing marker. An alternative method is lightly spraying fabric with water, and dusting talc powder into lines of stencil.

3. Attach darning foot to sewing machine. Drop feed dogs or cover feed dogs with a plate. No stitch length is required as you control the length. Use a fine needle and invisible or regular thread in the top and regular thread to match the Backing in the bobbin. Loosen top tension if using invisible thread.

4. Place hands flat on sides of marking. Bring bobbin thread up on line. Lock stitch and clip thread tails. Free motion stitch around design. Lock stitches and cut threads.

Binding

1. Square off selvage edges, and sew 3" Binding strips together lengthwise. Fold and press in half with wrong sides together.

2. Place walking foot attachment on sewing machine and regular thread on top and in bobbin to match Binding.

3. Line up raw edges of folded Binding with raw edges of quilt in middle of one side. Begin stitching 4" from end of Binding. Sew with 10 stitches per inch, or 3.0 to 3.5. Sew ⅜" from edge, or width of walking foot.

4. Place pin ⅜" from corner.

5. At corner, stop stitching on pin ⅜" in from edge with needle in fabric. Remove pin. Raise presser foot and turn quilt toward corner.

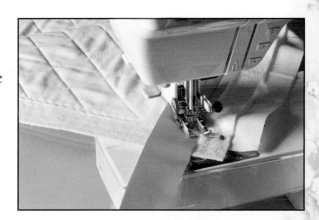

6. Put foot back down. Stitch diagonally off edge of Binding.

7. Raise foot, and pull quilt forward slightly. Turn quilt to next side.

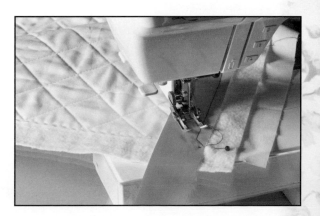

8. Fold Binding strip straight up on diagonal. Fingerpress diagonal fold.

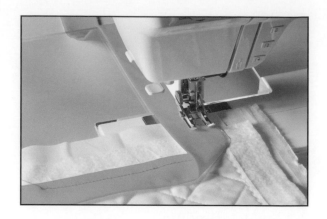

9. Fold Binding strip straight down with diagonal fold underneath. Line up top of fold with raw edge of Binding underneath.

10. Begin sewing from edge.

11. Continue stitching and mitering corners around outside of quilt.

12. Stop stitching 4" from where ends will overlap.

13. Line up two ends of Binding. Trim excess with ½" overlap.

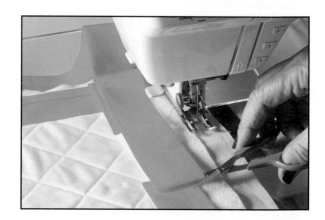

14. Open out folded ends and pin right sides together. Sew a ¼" seam. Press open seam.

15. Continue stitching Binding in place.

16. Trim Batting and Backing up to ⅛" from raw edges of Binding.

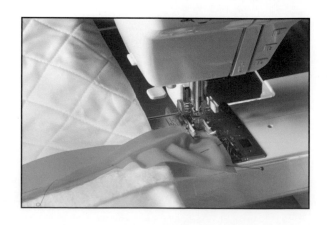

17. Fold back Binding.

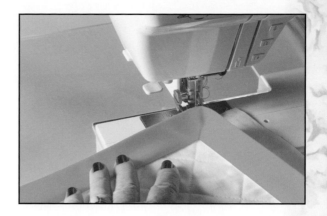

18. Pull Binding to back side of quilt. Pin in place so that folded edge on Binding covers stitching line. Tuck in excess fabric at each miter on diagonal.

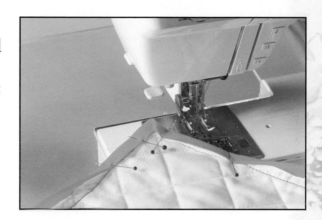

19. From right side, "stitch in the ditch" using invisible thread on front side, and bobbin thread to match Binding on back side. Catch folded edge of Binding on the back side with stitching.

Optional: Hand stitch Binding in place.

20. Hand stitch miter.

21. Sew identification label on Back.

- name of maker
- place where quilt was made
- year
- name of quilt
- any other pertinent information.

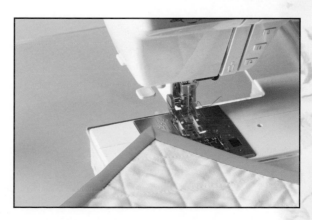

Index

Order Information

Quilt in a Day books offer a wide range of techniques and are directed toward a variety of skill levels. If you do not have a quilt shop in your area, you may write or call for a complete catalog and current price list of all books and patterns published by Quilt in a Day®, Inc.

Best Sellers

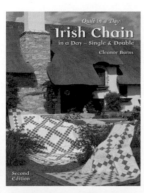  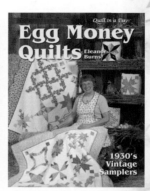 (top row)

 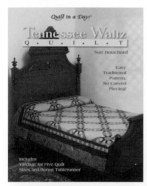 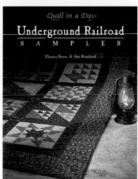  

Acknowledgements *A Heartfelt Thanks to these Hard Working Gals!*

Designers and Quiltmakers
Sue Bouchard
Angela Castro
Marie Harper
Patricia Knoechel
Mackie
Linda Parker
Bette Rhodaback
Aiko Rogers
Teresa Varnes
Pat Wetzel

Proofreaders
Sondra Grey
Mary Devendorf

Pattern Testers
Beverly Burris
Linda DeSaverio
Arlette Cheramie
Marty Halus
Peggy Stinson
Mary Westphal
And all my students!

Long Arm Quilters
Judy Jackson
Janna Mitchell
Amie Potter
Carol Selepec

Quilt in a Day®, Inc. • 1955 Diamond Street • San Marcos, CA 92078
800 777-4852 • Fax: 760 591-4424 • www.quiltinaday.com

Summer

Pink Lemonade

Teresa fussy cut medium-scale floral bouquets for her center squares and framed them in pink and white checks. The large-scale stripe outside border provides the perfect finish.

Pieced by Teresa Varnes
Quilted by Jana Mitchell